...ture made ... ty-
...ch one thousand nine hun-
...Between Thomas Floyd
...ich Road Ealing Middlesex
...einafter called the Lessor
...and Thomas Skurray
...d Abingdon Berks Brewer
...ed the Lessee of the other part
...at the Lessor doth hereby
...the Lessee All that piece
...in the Parish of Fritford
...Upper Heath containing
...or thereabouts Together

FRILFORD HEATH
GOLF CLUB

1908 - 2008
Celebrating a Century of Golf

Copyright © The Frilford Heath Golf Club Limited
Editor - Steven Baxter

ISBN 0-9558027-0-6

First published in England in 2007 by The Frilford Heath Golf Club Limited
Frilford, Abingdon, Oxfordshire, OX13 5NW

Printed by Wayzgoose Ltd.

Cover: Cyril Tolley and Roger Wethered playing an exhibition match at Frilford Heath in 1920

FRILFORD HEATH GOLF CLUB

1908 - 2008
Celebrating a Century of Golf

Compiled by Steven Baxter
Design Colin Reiners
Alice Tillotson

The Frilford Heath Golf Club Limited
Frilford Heath, Abingdon,
Oxfordshire, OX13 5NW

Contents

Preface and author's introduction

I have been privileged to have been asked to compile this club history. The task has been a fascination to me and has extended my love of the history of the game of golf and of Frilford Heath Golf Club in particular.

Many of our members will have seen the photograph of the fire in the thatched clubhouse in 1921, which resulted in its total loss. Before research began in earnest, I was convinced that there would consequently be a complete lack of records for the early and formative years of the Club. Not so, to my astonishment, initial ferreting around in the Committee Room revealed a complete run of General Committee minutes from 11 January 1913 to date. Sadly no minutes survive for the first few years of the Club, it is apparent that the constitution and management of the Club was only formalised when the Limited Company was formed a few years after golf had started at Frilford Heath. Perhaps earlier minutes never existed? What we now know of the very early years of the Club has been established from a review of the newspaper articles and golf magazines published at the time. A good deal of the later history has come from a careful review of the minutes which were thankfully meticulously kept by Club secretaries even during the difficult war years.

To research, write and then publish a history on this scale was a daunting task. It soon became clear to me that the only way to ensure a comprehensive readable book, was to enlist the help of others who had a wealth of information ready to be shared. Consequently I have been helped by a number of people to whom I extend my hearty thanks. In particular I thank the following, who have assisted with the research and drafting of some of the chapters - Sid Arrowsmith, Chris Allan, Paul Bence, Alistair Booth, Len Carrie, Mike Chapman, Clem Davies, Susan Erskine, Jim Franklin, Simon Gidman, Margaret Glennie, Peter McEvoy, Mary Normington, David Richards, Joe Skelton, Dick Stevens, Steve Styles and Paddy Viney.

The photographs, scans and other images are an important aspect of this book. Thanks to David Manson for organising the professional scanning of much old material, to Paul Sievers for the photographs of the trophies, Paul Sievers and Derek Walton for the photographs of the course, to Shamus Donald and Chris McDowell of the Oxford Mail and Times for providing a number of old newspaper photographs, to Sky Eye Aerial Photography Ltd for the new image of the clubhouse, to Julian P Graham Historical Photographic Collection for the images of Cyril Tolley and to a number of members who have provided their personal images for use in this book. Every effort has been made to contact copyright owners and the club will be pleased to hear from anyone who has inadvertently not been approached.

There is a distinctive character to this book with an impressive use of images from every one of the last ten decades. The design of the book is the work of Colin Reiners, a designer and photographer, graduate of the Royal College of Art and a Principal Lecturer at the University of Lincoln. Many thanks Colin, without your help this book just wouldn't be such a professional publication. Final thanks go to John Skeet and Alice Tillotson from the printers Wayzgoose Ltd who have worked tirelessly to interpret our ideas and produce this work for us.

Steven Baxter

Foreward

I am delighted and honoured to introduce the 100-year story of Frilford Heath Golf Club, tirelessly researched by Steven Baxter (a Director and Company Secretary) and his colleagues.

Having been weaned on links golf as a teenager and young man it was a joy to be introduced to Frilford Heath Golf Club over 50 years ago; a heathland golf course with many of the characteristics of links golf, in that, the fairways, being sandy by nature, were inevitably fast and bumpy. This, of course, was before fairway or even automatic green watering and now with these developments, both essential due to the greater level of play today, the heathland nature has, to a certain extent, disappeared.

We are fortunate, however, to have three 18-hole courses that are gold ranked in the top 100 courses in the country and in constant demand by the English Golf Union and the Ladies Golf Union for a variety of their tournaments. In fact, in our centenary year, the England v France match will be returning to Frilford Heath.

Over the years, we have supplied the BB & O County Team with many fine golfers, a scratch team captain in Sam Bowles in 1962 and 1963 and a County President in Myles Boddington, who later became President of the English Golf Union. Our finest achievement was when Richard Eyles represented England in the Walker Cup in 1975. Richard continues to be a member of Frilford Heath.

We have many reasons to thank the relatively small group of Abingdon golfing enthusiasts who, at the beginning of the 20th century identified the land at Frilford Heath as ideal for a golf course and set about acquiring it. To enable them to complete this and build an 18-hole golf course and pavilion clubhouse, they had to find the financial resources and The Frilford Heath Golf Club Limited was formed for this purpose.

Reaching 100 years is no small feat and I am very happy to have been a member for half that time and Chairman for 21 years, during which time many developments have taken place, hopefully for the benefit of members and visitors alike.

Joseph O. Skelton
Company Chairman
1986-2007

Foreword by the Centenary Captain

2008 - The year ahead

To be asked to be the Captain of such a prestigious Club as we have here at Frilford Heath is a great honour and privilege, and to be the Club Captain for the centenary year is something incredibly special that will give me immeasurable pleasure.

The stature of Frilford Heath, with its 54 holes, has brought challenging golf to members and visitors alike over the past 100 years. The club has played host to national and international amateur events and will do so again in May 2008 with the return of the England v France International. The PGA EuroPro Tour has now made Frilford Heath Golf Club its first port of call in its year due to the excellence of the tees, greens and fairways so early in the season, and in April 2008 we will again be hosting this event.

For Frilford Heath Golf Club members (male, ladies and juniors) we will be running all our usual annual knockouts and competitions with the 'majors' (as some members refer to them) being fought for keenly. Who will get their name on the winners' boards in this our centenary year?

Particularly exciting events will be the Festival and Gala weeks of golf to be held during the middle two weeks of August. During the Festival week there will be a series of Opens for guests to come and enjoy the delights of Frilford's courses, hospitality and food. During the Gala week, members will be able to invite a guest to play in various competitions for no charge. This gesture from the club is by way of a thank you to members for their contribution to the life of Frilford Heath Golf Club over the years. The week will culminate on the final Saturday with a stableford competition for men, ladies and juniors, when the first centenary trophies will be won. However, the winners will not be able to keep them for the next 100 years as these will become annual competitions! On this final day of the two weeks we will have the prize giving in the evening, followed by a barbeque and entertainment. I am sure that our centenary project, The Skelton Room, will be well used during this period.

On the social front, your committee has, as always, come up with an array of functions to be held during the year. These will allow us to enjoy the facilities of Frilford Heath Golf Club to the full, as well as the superb food that Stuart, Mandy and their staff provide.

11

However, the main social event, The Official Centenary Celebration dinner, will have to be held off site as we anticipate 300 guests, including members, guests and VIPs. We are taking advantage of the wonderful facilities at Christ Church in Oxford where, on 12 April, we will have a black tie gala dinner with entertainment when we will officially recognise 100 years of golf at Frilford Heath.

I do hope that you will join me and enjoy the extensive programme of celebration and golf that has been planned for our centenary.
As we reflect on the past and look forward to the future, we should be thankful for the memories we have of Frilford Heath Golf Club and play our part in its future.

Alistair Booth

Introduction

My first memories of Frilford Heath are of playing in the Golf Medal in the early 1970s in scorching weather. These were embryonic years for me in golfing terms and I never really challenged for the Medal itself, but it was one of my first experiences of high quality amateur golf.

I also remember this experience for putting on what remains one of the two fastest greens I have ever putted on. The other was the 1st green at Royal Birkdale in the first round of the 1976 Open. That same year, and during a drought, it was the 17th green on the Green course. I only had a 6 foot putt, which I holed, but my playing partner and I amused ourselves with a few practice putts where the ball was nearly free rolling on a parched flat area around the hole. It would have been 15 feet on a stimpmeter (if they had invented the stimpmeter!). Many courses experienced extremes during that dry summer but this was most unusual.

I loved the courses and still feel the same; it is God-given golfing land - sandy and firm. There are a great variety of holes on the three courses and a plethora of that much neglected genre, short par 4s. In the modern era with its obsession with power, designers often overlook such holes. Frilford Heath has some of the very best, especially on the Green course.

Once my career had advanced a little I had the honour of representing England in a match against France in 1984. I played in the first foursomes with Craig Lawrence who was English Champion at the time.

We decided Craig should hit off the first tee. A good crowd collected to watch his opening shot. Craig was an excellent driver but on this occasion hit three inches behind the ball and I played our second shot from the down slope at the end of the tee.

Frilford Heath was well known for more than its wonderful courses. Richard Eyles was a member and a top amateur in the mid 1970s. He played a Walker Cup at St Andrews and also an Eisenhower Trophy representing Great Britain and Ireland. I didn't play all that often with Richard but a practice round at Royal Lytham when he was at his peak sticks in my mind. It was quite evident how far ahead of the rest of us he was at that time.

On the administration side, Myles Boddington was a major figure when I was playing internationally. A great contributor and companion – he did a lot for English golf.

So Frilford Heath Golf Club always seemed to be there - part of the scene. It was somewhere you always looked forward to visiting. And it remains the same today. Although my early memories are of hot, sunny days at the Gold Medal, I actually love to play the courses in the winter months. Their dryness, especially compared with most other courses, distances Frilford Heath Golf Club from others and gives a welcome break from the mud.

Congratulations on your centenary, you are a fine club.

Peter McEvoy OBE

CENTENARY 1908 - 2008

FRILFORD HEATH GOLF CLUB

How did it all begin?

For how long the 'Royal and Ancient' game has been played in Scotland is a constant subject for debate among golfing historians. As far as England is concerned, in the mid 1700s there was just one isolated club, at Blackheath near Greenwich. The game only slowly started to spread down into England with a handful of clubs being formed in the mid 19th century. The original golf course at Blackheath is now built over, so the oldest club in England still playing over their original links is Royal North Devon which was formed in 1864. This was closely followed by Royal Wimbledon (1865) and Royal Liverpool at Hoylake (1869). Ten years later, there were still only a dozen or so golf clubs in England, but from about 1885 onwards, the game became fashionable throughout the country and golf really started to take off.

By the end of the 19th century, the game was well established among the gentry. Golf was now featuring alongside the other traditional pastimes of fishing and shooting. The catalyst is not certain, but a factor was certainly the growth of the railways and, as a consequence, the development of seaside holiday towns. The game was coming within the reach of more than just the upper class gentry. In the last decade of the 19th century, golf was fast growing in popularity. In the late 1880s and the 1890s more than 500 new clubs were formed, with a similar explosion in formations in the early 1900s up to the outbreak of the First World War.

What of golf in Oxfordshire in 1908? Golf in the county undoubtedly started with the University. The Oxford University Golf Club was formed in 1875 and the members played on a course over Cowley Marsh. This is the home of the present day Oxford City Golf Club, which was formed in 1899 and still now shares the course with the Oxford University Golf Club. Other clubs formed at about this time were

Chipping Norton	1890
Goring and Streatley	1895
Huntercombe	1901
North Oxford	1907
Henley	1907

Typical golfing attire when the Club was formed? – A card posted in 1908.

One Difficulty of the Game – Keeping your eye on the ball.

18

When the Frilford Heath Golf Club moved to the present clubhouse in the 1960s, Sydney Cullen wrote a short article for the benefit of the members. His notes on the early days are very informative and are partly reproduced below.

A picture of the first clubhouse taken within a few years of the Club's formation and before the 1921 fire – of which more in a later Chapter.

"It all began in the 1890s when the members of some of the more prominent Abingdon families amused themselves after Sunday lunch with a little chipping and putting on their lawns. One of these houses was the Abbey House, then the Palace of the Bishop of Reading, but whether his lordship took part we are not informed.

However, by the turn of the century, sufficient interest was aroused to form a club and rent two fields on the Wootton Road (where the Council estate and School of Further Education now stand) where a nine hole golf course was constructed.

After a few years, the Club moved to Shippon where they were tenants of the Duchy of Cornwall on a much more commodious parcel of land. But all the time there lay, about 3 miles west of Abingdon, one of those odd stretches of land, intended by nature for a golf course, but hitherto unrecognised. Poor and shallow sandy soil of little agricultural use where gorse and heather were indigenous, and over the centuries a little stone and some peat had been extracted, of course, a golfer's paradise."

The Club in Abingdon to which Sydney Cullen refers is the North Berks Golf Club which was based on land in Shippon, subsequently built over for RAF Abingdon, and now the Army barracks. That Club must have played over far less suitable land and struggled to maintain

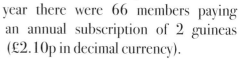

putting on the present 4th on the Green course - crossroads in view in the background

local interest in the game. As a consequence, membership numbers were probably unviable and finances always difficult to balance.

The Club has in its possession a leather-bound membership record for the North Berks Golf Club which starts in January 1902. For that year there were 66 members paying an annual subscription of 2 guineas (£2.10p in decimal currency).

The Abingdon Herald of Saturday 22 May 1909 reports on the exhibition match held on the official opening of Frilford Heath Golf Club, a match between Harry Vardon and J H Taylor. The article states:

"On the threatened eviction of the North Berks Golf Club from Shippon last year, to make room for small holdings, a small syndicate of the members acquired leases of about 150 acres of waste lands on Frilford Heath, belonging to Magdalen College and other owners, and an army of labourers has been

A match during 1913

engaged during the past Autumn and Winter, under the supervision of the local professional (A Pedler), in converting these into what bids fair to become one of the finest inland courses in the country.

The pretty little thatched club room from Shippon has been enlarged and re-erected at Frilford, and redecorated, and a site has been secured for a more elaborate club house, should it be found desirable to build one later on."

So what became of the golf club at Shippon? The article in The Abingdon Herald certainly gives the impression that the club folded at about the time that Frilford Heath Golf Club was formed. How could it continue to exist if it had sold its club house? But, some present day members remember the Shippon course still being in existence and being played over a good many years later. Perhaps the club reformed at a later date and played again over that land.

Frilford Heath Golf Club was formed in early 1908. Unfortunately committee minute books only start in 1912 (when the Club became a limited company), so detailed information regarding the formation of the Club and the early years is hard to come by. The Club does have in its possession the original leases for the land. The leases are signed on 31 March 1908, so failing any information to the contrary, we can take that as the date on which our Club was formed.

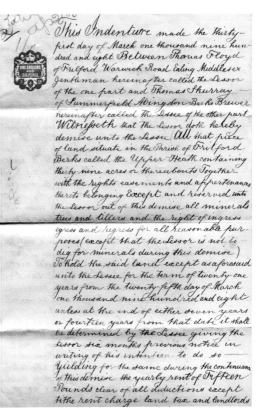

The original 18-hole course

How was our course perceived by our predecessors, those Edwardian golfers who played regularly or occasionally visited Frilford Heath? Fortunately we have some descriptions of the course, which are reproduced below. Then, at the end of the chapter, for the benefit of members, there is a hole by hole description of the original course as it was played; some of the holes being almost exactly as they are today.

Nisbet's Golf Year Book was the golfers' handbook produced annually in the early 1900s. The 1911 handbook describes the club as follows:

Frilford Heath, near Abingdon (Berkshire)

Frilford Heath Golf Club (formerly North Berks Golf Club)
Inst. 1909
Number of members – 142
Stations – Abindon (GWR) 3¼ miles, Oxford 6 miles, Wantage 6 miles
Hon. Sec. – A E Preston, Whitefields, Abingdon
Assistant Sec. – E J Jones, Dog House Hotel, Abingdon
Entrance Fee - £5 5s. Subs - £3 3s.
Number of holes – 18
Pro – A Pedlar
Amateur record – Captain Adair, 76
Professional record – H Vardon, 74
Terms for visitors – 2s. 6d. per day; 10s per week; 20s per month
Ladies may play by introduction of members only
Sunday play, without caddies

The course was laid out by J H Taylor (ex Open Champion), and is one of the finest inland links in England. The turf is magnificent and of the seaside variety, the subsoil being sand throughout. The 18 holes represent over 6000 yards' play, with several sporting short holes. There are excellent natural hazards, some supplying heroic carries, in addition to large and well placed bunkers in the deep sand.

The Abingdon Herald (22 May 1909)

A description of the course was given in The Abingdon Herald of 22 May 1909, when the opening exhibition match was reported.

The course is a long one (6118 yards), three of the holes being over 500 yards in length. On the threatened eviction of the North Berks Club from Shippon, last year, to make room for smallholdings, a small syndicate of the members acquired leases of about 150 acres of waste lands on Frilford Heath, and an army of labourers has been employed during the past autumn and winter, under the superintendence of the local professional (A Pedlar), in converting these into what bids fair to become one of the finest inland golf courses in the country. The sandy soil at Frilford Heath produces a growth of turf of a kind usually found only amongst the sand hills on the sea coast, and such turf is peculiarly adapted to golfing. The numerous bunkers are filled with the pure natural sand, found about a foot or so below the surface, which is quite free from stones, and simply has to be exposed to form the most perfect possible hazards. Gorse and heather are found all over the course, but are kept within such limits as to reduce the chances of actual loss of balls to a minimum. The course was laid out by J H Taylor, and has been very skilfully arranged, so as to make the greatest possible use of the many natural hazards afforded by the peculiarities of the ground. Amongst these the most noticeable are the Blackwater Brook (which is crossed at the 3rd, 7th, 11th and 17th), two old stone pits guarding the 9th, and a vast sand pit (which has been called 'The Acre Bunker' in front of the 8th green. There are three excellent short holes , the 7th, (115 yards), the 13th (132 yards), where the green is practically surrounded by sand bunkers, and the 15th (110 yards), where the mashie shot from the tee must be dead straight to avoid the ring of gorse bushes closing in the green. A feature of the course is the placing of the 9th and 18th greens close to the site of the club house. This enables competitions or matches to be started simultaneously from the 1st and 10th tees, and has the additional advantage on windy days of giving players a few holes alternately with and against the wind, instead of having, as is often the case in any wind swept seaside courses, to slog out for nine holes in the teeth of a gale and return home for the remaining nine holes with a following wind.

Golf courses of the British Isles by Bernard Darwin (1910)

Golf course guide books abound nowadays, but 100 years ago they were few and far between. One of the most respected golf writers of the time was Bernard Darwin. He wrote a guide to golf in the British Isles that has become one of the classics, which any golf book collector wants to have in his collection. Chapter VIII is entitled 'Oxford and Cambridge', and the first half of this chapter is reproduced in full below because it gives a fascinating insight into golf in the area, as well as a fine description of Frilford Heath.

───────────────

"The Universities of Oxford and Cambridge are rich in many things, but are very decidedly poor in the matter of golf courses. I should be more precise if I said poor in their own courses, for in Frilford Heath and Worlington (or as it is often called, Mildenhall) they are lucky to possess hospitable neighbours, who provide them with very delightful golf indeed.

The short seventh
(now the 2nd Green course)

The courses of Cambridge I know very well indeed, having played over them at intervals during the greater part of my life. With those of Oxford I have only, comparatively speaking, a bowing acquaintance, founded on the annual match between the University and the Oxford and Cambridge Golfing Society. Before turning to Frilford there is a word to be said of Cowley, Radley and Hinksey. The latter of which has now ceased to exist. Cowley, so I have heard my friend Mr Croome declare, is now rather a good course, and as I have never seen it, I most certainly will not venture to contradict him; but I can take my oath as to both Hinksey and Radley that they call for some other epithet. Hinksey was certainly amusing, and I have spent not wholly unpleasant afternoons there squelching

through the mud and trying vainly to hole putts by cannoning off alternate wormcasts. There was a short hole – the fourth, I think – where one played a pitching shot into the heart of a wood which was distinctly entertaining, but on the whole it was not a good test of golf, or, if it was, then I would rather have my golf tested in some other way.

When Hinksey ceased to exist Radley came into being, and it is most decidedly a longer and more difficult course, but I am not certain that it is such good fun. It is a good deal longer; indeed many of the holes are of a good length. There is a really good seventeenth, where one skirts a wood on the right, and granted a good lie – a thing which rests upon the knees of the

gods – one may hit two really fine shots and get a fine four. I imagine, however, that no one will be prepared to deny that it is muddy – I will go so far as to say extremely muddy – and in these days we are so pampered with beautiful sandy inland courses that we no longer suffer mud at all gladly. So if we are at Oxford I think we had better throw economy to the winds and charter a 'taxi', which shall take us up Cumnor Hill to Frilford Heath.

Frilford is only seven miles from Oxford, but it might be a hundred miles from anywhere. It lies on a little unfrequented by-road, and is as utterly rural and peaceful a spot as could be found anywhere. Here is sand enough and to spare – a wonderful oasis in the desert of mud. The sand is so near the turf that out of pure exuberance it breaks out here and there in little eruptions on the surface or flies up in a miniature sand-storm as the ball alights. The ground is for the most part very flat, and there are fir trees and whins [gorse bushes] scattered here and there. There is also a pretty wood of firs and birches, over which we have to drive at the third hole, of which more anon. The greens are a little rough as yet, and some of the bunkers have still to be made, or at least had not been made when I last played there; but time alone is wanted to make Frilford a very fine course indeed. It is already a wonderfully charming one.

The first two holes remind one a little of

Fifth green - (the first green on the Red until the Blue course alterations, now taken out of play but still exists)

26

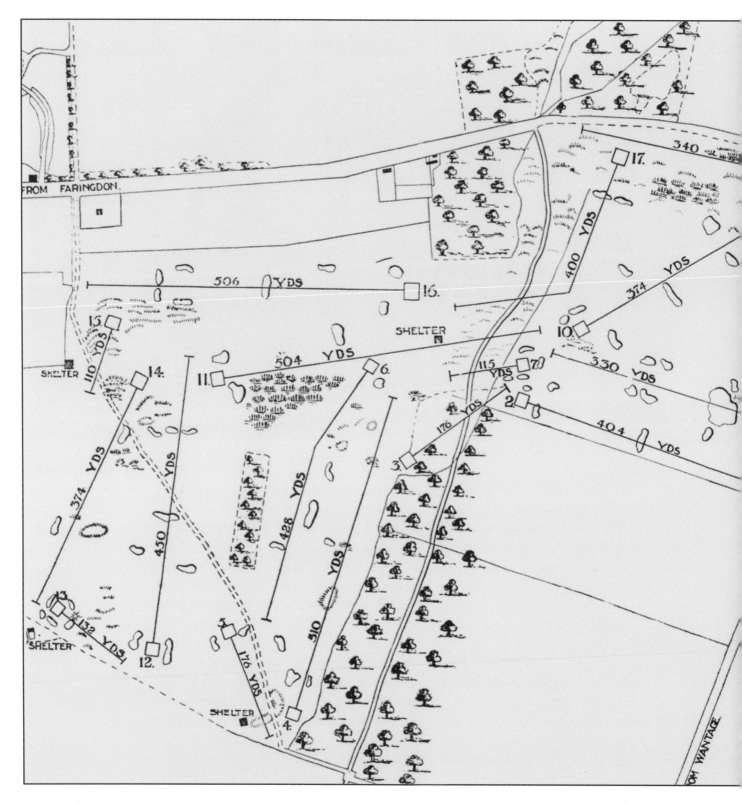

FROM FARINGDON.

340

17.

506 YDS 16.

400 YDS

374 YDS

15 110 YDS

SHELTER

SHELTER

504 YDS

6.

115 YDS 7.

10.

330 YDS

14.

11.

2.

404 YDS

374 YDS

450 YDS

428 YDS

176 YDS

3.

310 YDS

13

132 YDS

SHELTER

12.

5.

176 YDS

SHELTER

4.

FROM WANTAGE.

FRILFORD HEATH GOLF LINKS.

Muirfield, since there is a stone wall over which a pulled ball will inevitably vanish. The second is a fine long two-shot hole, and at the first, which is somewhat shorter, a highly ingenious use has been made of a solitary tree, which forces the player to drive close to the stone wall if he is to have an open approach. Then comes the third before mentioned, which is a one-shot hole. The wood rises pretty steeply in front of the tee, and the shot is made the more difficult because a cleek is hardly long enough, and so we have to take a wooden club. Many a shot that would under ordinary circumstances fill us with a mild degree of conceit will only send the ball crashing into the forest. It is no hole for the 'low racker' which we regard with complacency at Hoylake and St Andrews. We must hit a fine towering shot, and then we may hope to find our ball on the green – a pretty little green which nestles close to the lee of the wood on the far side. After this come some long open holes in a country of scattered whin bushes. Exactly how long they are I am not prepared to say. I played them in the company of Mr A J Evans, and he appeared to regard them justifiably as two-shot holes, but personally I found myself taking by no means the most lofted of my iron clubs for my third shot. There is a pretty little pitching hole over a stone wall – the seventh – which has a flavour of Harlech about it; and the ninth, which brings us close to the clubhouse again, is surely one of the most alarming holes in existence. The drive is simple enough, but my goodness, what a second! In front of the green is a mountain, and on either side of the green are deep pits, towards which the ground 'draws' most unmistakably. Then the green itself is quite small, and has in its centre a copy of the aforesaid mountain in miniature. The approach shot, moreover, is by no mean a short one, but is for the ordinary driver a good firm iron shot, so that a four is really an epoc-making score for the hole.

After the turn it seems to me that the golf shows a distinct falling off. The holes are still long enough, and Mr Evans still seemed to require one stroke less to reach the green than I did, but for the most part they lack the indefinable charm of the first nine. There is, however, certainly one exception to this general criticism, and that is the really fascinating seventeenth, which is emphatically the right hole in the right place. There is a wood and a stone wall to carry, and the angle at which we play is such that there is a very real reward for the long ball which is judiciously hooked. A good, as opposed to an ordinary, drive may make all the difference between a four and a five, for the green is full of undulations, and the nearer we are to it when we take our iron in hand the better.

Taking it altogether the golf is both good and difficult, and besides that Frilford is essentially one of those places where it is good to be alive with a golf club in one's hand – even if one uses it indifferently – and whither one looks forward to returning with a very keen enjoyment."

Cowley – *is the course we now refer to as Southfield, home of Oxford City Golf Club.*
Hinksey – *this course was very close to the present Hinksey Heights Golf Club, centred around Chilswell Farm which is about a mile off the road to Boars Hill from Hinksey Hill.*
Radley – *not to be confused with the present day Radley College course. Radley Parish extends into parts of what we now consider to be Kennington. The clubhouse was situated near to the shops in the Playfield Road area of Kennington and the area over which golf was played is mostly covered in housing now. The club never reopened after being closed during the First World War.*

The ninth green (now forth on Green course) with original thatched clubhouse in the background

The layout of the original course in 1908

The original clubhouse was situated in the northwest corner of the crossroads of the Wantage and Tubney roads. The crossroads were, at that time, a straight crossing of the two roads. This crossroads later became very dangerous. The County Council purchased an area of land from the Club in the early 1970s, soon after the Club had moved to the present clubhouse. This allowed the old clubhouse to be demolished and the Tubney Road to be rerouted, creating its gentle curve and making the junction safer. The small, but adequate, car park was immediately behind the clubhouse and is still present as the occasional car park behind the tee of the 5th on the Green course.

The old clubhouse sat right in the middle of the present roadway and golfers had to cross the road to reach the 1st tee. At this time there were just 18 holes at Frilford Heath; the nine holes we know as 'the short nine' of the Green course were added in the late 1920s.

Many of the original 18 holes are played today, others were lost when the courses were extended from 27 to 36 holes at the time the Club moved to Frilford House. What follows is a description of the original holes built in 1908. One par 3 hole was removed in 1921 and replaced with another par 3, so 19 holes are described below.

Hole 1 (392 yards)
This hole was the present 14th on the Green course. The hole was played from the present yellow tee. The back tee used for the present hole would have been pretty much in the middle of the present crossroads!

Hole 2 (404 yards)
This hole was the present 15th on the Green course.

Hole 3 (176 yards)
This par 3 was very controversial and unloved. It played from behind the present 15th green on the Green course up towards the present 16th yellow tee. The shot had to be played over a copse of trees. The hole was probably the only badly designed hole on the course and was abandoned in 1921. The replacement hole is described below as some older members will remember all but the original third.

Hole 4 (510 yards)
The tee for this hole was just outside the bend of the present path from the 15th green to the 16th tee on the Green course, where its rear left 'shoulder' can just be seen. The hole ran from this tee to the present 8th green on the Red course. All along the left of this hole, at that time, was a wood. The land was part of

This view gives a good idea of the general character of the course in the early years. This is the 10th green (now 15th on Red) with 8th fairway beyond (now 3rd on Green).

30

the estate surrounding Frilford House later purchased by the club. On this land are all or a part of the present 1st, 16th, 17th, and 18th holes of the Green course, and all or part of the 1st, 9th, 10th, 17th and 18th of the Red course.

Hole 4 (298 yards) (added in 1929 to replace hole 3 above)

This short par 4 continued roughly in the direction of the previous hole. The front of one of its tees can still be seen protruding from the gorse bushes to the right of the rough about 25 paces short and to the right of the sycamore tree on the left of the hill to the right of the present 1st of the Red course.

Hole 5 (176 yards)

This hole was played from a tee in the rough to the right of what is now the fairway of the 10th Blue course, to approximately the green formerly used for the present 1st of the Red course.

Hole 6 (428 yards)

The tees for this dog-leg to the right hole can still be seen on a line joining approximately the present 7th tee on the Red and the 8th fairway of the Red. The tee is 25 yards into the rough just greenside of the hawthorn tree to the right of the 8th of the Red course, 100 yards short of the green. The fairway ran obliquely over the fairways of the present 8th, 10th and 17th of the Red course and the green was the present 1st of the Green course.

Hole 7 (115 yards)

This was the present 2nd hole on the Green course, but it was a considerably shorter hole. The original tee was just in front of Blackwater Brook.

THE CARRY FROM

33

Hole 8 (330 yards)

This was the present 3rd hole on the Green course.

Hole 9 (345 yards)

This was the present 4th hole on the Green course. This hole therefore brought the golfer back to the Tubney Road and the clubhouse.

Hole 10 (374 yards)

This was the present 15th hole on the Red course, but was somewhat shorter originally.

Hole 11 (504 yards)

This par 5 used the present 'winter' tee of the 16th on the Red course and used the left part of the present fairway for this hole. It continued on to the present 7th green of the Red course. The green was then in a significant hollow.

Hole 12 (450 yards)

The tees lay to the left of present 7th green of the Red course. Play was from here across what is now thick gorse to join the left part of the present 6th fairway of the Red course. The bunker on the right of the present 6th Red to catch tee shots is new, but the fairway cross bunkers are original features. The green was the present 6th green of the Red course.

Hole 13 (138 yards)

This short hole has completely disappeared. The tee was situated in a cutting in the trees, which lie beyond and to the right of the 6th of the Red course. The green lay immediately to the right of the path leading from the present green on the 4th Red course to the 5th tee of the Red course. The path is the position of a long bunker, which lay just over the green.

Hole 14 (374 yards)

The tee was roughly where the ladies tee for the 2nd on the Red course is now. The hole crossed the present 5th fairway of the Red course obliquely from left to right, to a green situated in the rough between the present 5th fairway and 6th tee of the Red course. A cross bunker was present on this hole about 60 yards short of the green but on the site of the present group of gorse bushes to the right of the present cross bunker.

Hole 15 (110 yards)

The green for this hole is the present 5th green of the Red course. The original tee for this hole was in the rough, approximately to the left of the present 5th Red fairway cross bunker.

Hole 16 (506 yards)

This was the present 12th hole on the Red course. The present hole is some 30 yards shorter than that of the original layout. The tees could not have been further back than they are at the moment so it is assumed that the original green was further towards the woods than the green we use today.

Hole 17 (400 yards)

This was the present 13th hole on the Red course. Again, this hole was longer than we play it now. The green is the original and the tees don't appear to have been further back than they are now, so presumably the hole was measured as more of a dog-leg than it is measured now. Where the cross bunker is off the tee, there was a low stone wall, removed some time ago.

Hole 18 (340 yards)

This was the present 14th hole on the Red course, which therefore took our Edwardian golfers back to the clubhouse.

A G Barry (1905 Amateur champion) playing at Frilford Heath in 1913.

1909 exhibition match officially opens the course

We have not been able to establish precisely when golf was first played over the new links at Frilford. Undoubtedly for a good part of 1908, the holes were under construction. At this time golf course construction was not as complex as it is now; much was made of the land as it lay, without vast amounts of earth being moved to shape fairways. Golf would certainly have been possible towards the end of the year. From early in the 1909 season the course was surely fully established.

Exhibition matches were an important part of the golfing scene, with clubs wishing to promote their facilities by bringing the game to golfers and spectators from the local area. Frilford Heath Golf Club was of course no exception. In fact when the club became a limited company on 25 November 1912 one of the stated objectives of the company was to arrange such exhibition matches.

To promote and hold competitions and matches in connection with Golf and to contribute to prizes, medals, cups, testimonials, and other rewards and to arrange and pay for exhibition matches and competitions between professionals and to promote give or support luncheons, dinners, concerts and other entertainments.'

Thus it was that the Club held a most prestigious match in May 1909 between two of the greatest golfers of the time, Harry Vardon and J H Taylor. The event was fully reported in The Abingdon Herald of 22 May 1909. The report is such an interesting piece that it is reproduced in part below.

'The formal opening of the 18-hole golf course at Frilford Heath took place on Friday the 14th inst., when an exhibition match of 36 holes was played by the two well known professionals and ex open champions, Harry Vardon of Totteridge Park and J H Taylor of Richmond.

The pretty little thatched club room from Shippon has been enlarged and re-erected at Frilford, and redecorated, and a site has been secured for a more elaborate club house, should it be found desirable to build one later on.

The opening match excited considerable interest in the neighbourhood, and before 11 o'clock a considerable crowd of visitors had arrived; parties of golfers and others not only from Oxford and Abingdon, but from Reading, Swindon, Wantage, Witney, Chipping Norton and other places in the neighbourhood. Doubts had been expressed as to whether Vardon, who had been playing in the final of the Open competition at St Andrew's, on the previous afternoon, would be able to get to Frilford in time. However, the sportsmanlike golfer at St Andrew's started his match there half-an-hour before time and kept a train waiting for him for ten minutes to enable him to catch the night mail to London. He accordingly turned up at Abingdon before 10 o'clock, looking as fresh as new paint, and as fit as well – Harry Vardon.

The match was started punctually at 11 o'clock, the Hon D Finch-Hatton, the captain of the Oxford University Golf Club, acting as referee. Taylor took the honour at the first tee, and when the little white ball was seen to roll steadily up towards the May bush, and stop about 270 yards from the tee, the spectators

realised that they were to see a veritable encounter of giants. Vardon's drive was about the same distance, but his second shot was slightly sliced and pitched over the bunker. Taylor's second shot was dead straight, but overran the green into rough, and the hole was halved in 5. At the second hole Taylor pulled his drive out of bounds, but got an excellent second from the tee, and laid his ball close to Vardon's , about half way to the green. Vardon played one of his marvellous iron shots to the green for 2, and Taylor, taking his brassie, also reached the green. Vardon was not up on his 3rd, but secured the hole with a 4 to Taylor's 5. Curiosity was roused at the 3rd hole, in view of recent newspaper correspondence, and those who resented it being called the one bad hole on the course were pleased to find that both players reached the green quite comfortably on the drive. We noticed a smile on the face of "One who was there". Both were short on the approach putt, and Vardon missed his 3rd, Taylor winning the hole with a 3 to his 4. The 4th hole afforded an excellent display of golf. Taylor's putt for a 4 hung on the lip of the tin, but he secured the hole for 5, Vardon having overrun the green into rough. The 5th was taken by Vardon for 3, Taylor playing 3 putts to hole out. At the 6th a curious incident occurred. Vardon, in playing his 2nd took too much ground, and his ball lodged in an overhanging branch of gorse, about 18 inches off the ground, but taking an iron club he struck it out as easily as though from a tee, and drove the ball about 70 yards, lodging it quite close to the green, but a little to the left.

J H Taylor and H Vardon - forth green

Taylor, however, laid his 3rd close to the flag and secured the hole 5¬6. The 7th, 8th, and 9th were halved in 3, 5 and 4, respectively. Taylor had a bit of bad luck at the 8th, where in playing his 4th for the hole he just lipped the hole and missed. On the 10th green Taylor missed a putt of about a yard for a half and lost the hole 5, 4. At the 11th Taylor got a bad lie for his second, but played a splendid iron shot out and halved the hole in 5. Vardon took the 12th with a 4 to Taylor's 5. At the 13th Taylor played a splendid mashie shot from the tee, and laid his ball within a yard of the flag, and secured the hole with a 2 to Vardon's 3. At the 14th Vardon played a grand 2nd on to the green. Taylor's 2nd landed him in the rough on the edge of the green, and he had to concede the hole to Vardon 5¬4. Taylor

again lipped (back). The 16th was halved in 5. At the 17th both drove a long ball well over the wall, but Vardon was short on his 3rd and 4th and Taylor won the hole 4¬5. At the 18th both players were in the rough on their drives, and Taylor, in playing out, narrowly escaped striking the newly appointed Hon. Secretary. Fortunately for the club, however, that officer, by a somewhat unwonted display of agility, managed to avoid the ball. Taylor lost the hole 5¬4, thus leaving the match all square at the end of the morning match.

The lessees entertained the players, the committee and stewards, and a few friends to luncheon in the club room. The Mayor of Abingdon (Mr H S Challenor) presided, and was supported by the Captain of the Club

a good crowd watches at the first tee of the exhibition match - J H Taylor has just driven, Vardon looking on

(Mr J T Morland) and others. Amongst others present we noticed Mr W H Fairbrother (Lincoln College), Dr Macan (the Master of the University, and President of the Oxford University Golf Club), Mr J A R Marriott (New College), the Rev T Layng, Mr A E Preston, Mr C A Pryce, Mr E J Harris, Mr B Challenor, Mr G Saxby, Mr T Skurray, Mr C Rippon, and the Hon. D Finch-Hatton (referee).

The committee, players, and stewards, etc., were photographed after luncheon by Mr Warland Andrew, of Abingdon, who took a series of photographs during the match.

The afternoon match started punctually at 3 o'clock, and produced a wonderful exhibition of golf. Taylor was playing quite a good game, but was beaten comparatively easily by Vardon, who subsequently admitted that he had never played a better round in his life. The 1st hole was halved in 4, Vardon being short in his putt. At the 2nd Taylor pulled his drive into the wall, and played out into a bunker, giving Vardon the hole in 4-6. The tees at the 3rd were again faultlessly carried by both players, and the hole was halved in 3. Taylor secured the 4th (4-5) after a short drive by Vardon. At the 5th Taylor drove into the bunker on the right of the green, and could only reach the edge of the green on playing out, but he laid the ball dead on the 5th, and managed to get a half in 4, as Vardon missed a comparatively easy putt. Vardon secured the 6th (4-5), Taylor having on his 3rd stroke down the hill overshot the hole. At the 7th both players drove onto the green, but Taylor missed his putt, and gave the hole to Vardon (2-3). On the 8th green Vardon successfully negotiated a putt of six yards to win the hole (3-4). At the 9th both

Back row: *E J Jones (Asst. Secretary), A Pedlar, A C M Croome, J H Taylor, Hon D Finch - Hatton, H Vardon, L W Daniell, Capt. M J Slade*

Middle row: *W H Fairbrother, C A Pryce, A E Preston (Hon. Secretary), H S Challenor (President), J T Morland,*
        H G W D'Almaine, T Skurray
Front row: *A Edmondson, C D Rotch, W D Mellersh, W T Morland, G W Shepherd*

THE GOLFER.

HARRY VARDON IN A WINNING VEIN.

FRILFORD HEATH.

DESPITE the fact that he had travelled throughout the night from Scotland, Harry Vardon played brilliant golf when he met J. H. Taylor in a match of thirty-six holes on the new course of the Frilford Heath club on Friday of last week. At the end of eighteen holes Taylor and Vardon were all even, each having a score of 78, but Vardon, showing magnificent form, went round in the afternoon in 70, and won by 5 and 3.

players drove into the bunker on the right, but Vardon played a grand shot onto the green, Taylor also played out with a fine shot, but got into trouble on the right of the green. A magnificent stroke out of the bank of the hazard, and a long putt, gave him, however, a half in 4. Both players were on the 10th green in 2, but 2 short putts by Taylor gave Vardon the hole (4-5). At the 11th Vardon missed a short putt, giving Taylor the hole in 4-5. A putt of four yards gave Vardon a half for 4 at the 12th. The 13th was halved in faultless style in 3. At the 14th Taylor played his second into gorse, and had to pick out, but Vardon played a grand 2nd long shot on to the green, and won the hole in 4-6, making him dormy 4. He secured the 15th in 3-4, thus winning the match 5 up and 3 to play. In the bye the 16th was won by Vardon (4-5), and the 17th and 18th by Taylor (4-5 at each hole). In driving at the 17th Vardon failed to carry the wall, but played a grand shot out of the rough for his 2nd. On the 18th green he missed a yard putt for the half.

There were of course a few disappointments. The clerk of the Meteorological Office should have arranged for the two good showers a week which Frilford Heath always wants to keep it in good condition. Instead of this they sent us no rain for three or four weeks prior to the match, and consequently the greens were not quite in such condition as they should have been. Despite this drawback, however, every one of the large crowd who followed the match appeared to be highly pleased with the course and the arrangements made by the committee, their Hon. Secretary (Mr A E Preston) and the Assistant (Mr E J Jones).

Estimates vary as to the number of spectators, but the general opinion seemed to be that about 500 people were present in the morning, and quite double that number in the afternoon. The crowd was very orderly, and their rather too eager desire to get a good and close view of every stroke did not require much repressing by the corps of flag wavers and stewards, who were instructed in their duties by Mr d'Almaine and Mr Fairbrother.

The subscription to the new club is to be £3 3s., with an entrance fee of £5 5s., but a limited number of members are to be admitted at the reduced fee of £4 4s., to cover entrance fee and subscription to the end of the current year. Applications for membership should be addressed to the Assistant Secretary, Mr E J Jones, Frilford Heath Golf Club, Abingdon.'

'Out of Africa'

What connection is there between the official opening of Frilford Heath Golf Club, a Danish Baroness, a Hollywood film and the Chairman of the company?

It sounds good enough for a Hercule Poirot plot, but that is not the answer. A previous Chapter reports the exhibition match in 1909 for the official opening of the course and includes the photograph taken that day to record the occasion. In the centre of the picture in the back row, standing between J H Taylor and Harry Vardon is Hon. D Finch-Hatton, who was an undergraduate at Oxford and a golfing blue.

After leaving Oxford University, Finch-Hatton travelled to Kenya. There he met and fell in love with an unhappily married Danish Baroness, Karen Blixen. She was endeavouring to start a coffee farm but was unsuccessful and eventually returned to Denmark. The affair between them is told in the 1985 film *'Out of Africa'*, with Meryl Streep as Karen and Robert Redford playing the part of Denys Finch-Hatton, a British aristocrat. Ironically, part of Karen Blixen's failed farm was later to become the best golf course in Kenya, named after her, The Karen Country Club.

Baroness Karen Blixen

And what is the connection with our Chairman Dick Stevens, well he was an extra in the film and appears on screen. For the film watchers among you, Dick appears at the end of the film when Karen (Meryl) is invited into the men's bar of Muthaiga Country Club following her bankruptcy.

Hon. D Finch-Hatton

Golf course architects
from 18 to 54 holes in 85 years

First, there is one common misconception that I must correct. We have a charming loop of nine holes in the middle of a round on the Green course, they are situated north of the Tubney Road and quite clearly were once a stand alone, nine-hole course. I have heard so many members refer to these nine holes as 'the original nine-hole golf course' but this is totally incorrect.

It is easy to see why this misconception arises. We can all still see the evidence of the site of the original clubhouse at the crossroads of Wantage Road and Tubney Road. The clubhouse was clearly on that side of the road and many members still recall when there were 27 holes at Frilford Heath. At that time, the main 18-hole course was situated between the crossroads and the present clubhouse and the other nine holes played as a separate loop of nine.

1908 – The original 18 holes

Quoting from a 1914 handbook:

A large tract of sandy ground, some 170 acres in extent, was discovered near Frilford,

Chronology of the creation of the various holes and the golf course architects involved

Year	Architect	Description	# Holes
1908	J H Taylor	Original 18-hole course over parts of the present Red and Green courses	18
1928	J H Turner	Nine-hole course added north of Tubney Road - the present holes 5 to 13 on the green course	27
1964	G K Cotton	After purchase of the present clubhouse and the land surrouding it a further nine holes were added. There were changes to a number of holes on the Red and Green courses to extend them to two 18-hole courses	36
1994	S Gidman	18-hole Blue course added, necessitating changes to holes 1 to 4 on Red course	54

which was apparently useless for ordinary agricultural purposes. It grew chiefly heather and gorse, and was the happy hunting ground of innumerable rabbits. The necessary leases were obtained, the rabbits exterminated, and the services of J H Taylor secured to lay out and supervise the construction of an 18-hole course.

J H Taylor (1871 – 1963), the architect of our original course was a very famous golfer indeed. When golfing at the turn of the century he was one of "the great triumvirate", three golfers who dominated competitive golf for a number of years. James Braid and Harry Vardon made up the trio. J H Taylor won the Open five times and many other tournaments.

J H Taylor served as professional at Westward Ho! for a number of years before moving to carry out similar duties at Burnham & Berrow, Winchester, Wimbledon and Royal Mid Surrey.

J H Taylor laid out a few golf courses before World War I, the first thought to be in 1905 so our course represents some of his earliest work. He was most prolific in the 1920's when much of his work was in partnership with the well renowned F G Hawtree.

It would be quite impossible nowadays, but J H Taylor managed to find the time to combine a full time job as a club professional, be an eminent designer of golf courses and play competitive golf at the highest level. It is difficult to imagine anyone managing to excel at more than one of these disciplines today, let alone all three!!

A much fuller description of the original 18-hole layout appears in a pevious chapter.

1928 – An additional nine holes

During his years at Frilford Heath, as the Club's Professional, J H Turner carried out a number of improvements to the original 18-hole layout. His greatest triumph though was the design and construction of the nine-hole course to the north of the Tubney Road. Frilford Heath Golf Club was so popular in the 1920s that this additional nine-hole course was developed to relieve the pressure on the 'old' course. It was in no sense a 'relief' course though; it was held in high regard.

John Henry Turner was a well known golfer and latterly golf club manufacturer. He is not particularly known as a golf club architect though and does not merit a mention in a leading reference manual, "The Architects of Golf". He was perhaps not involved in the creation of many other courses, though it is known that he designed the original 9 holes at Burford which opened for play in 1936, he remodelled Goring & Streatley in 1928 and also redesigned Newbury & Crookham.

The high esteem in which this course was held cannot be better illustrated than by quoting a

48

famous golf correspondent of the time. In the 1930s he wrote of the nine-hole course:

To find a course to compare with it one has to think very hard, and only the Royal Worlington comes to mind. I am not going to say which is the better but will confine myself by recording that Royal Worlington and Frilford Heath's second course are two of the best nine-hole courses in England. It is a coincidence that both are used from time to time by the University golfers of Cambridge and Oxford, respectively.

1967 – From 27 to 36 holes

The original Frilford Heath Golf Course was flanked on the south by the estate of Frilford Heath House. The directors were always concerned that this area might be developed to the detriment of the tranquil setting of the course. When the estate came on to the market, the Company purchased it, securing not only the house but also an additional 44 acres of land.

The services of C K Cotton were secured and a further nine holes were constructed. From this point onwards the Club benefited from two full 18-hole courses; those we know as the Red and Green courses.

Charles Kenneth Cotton (1887 – 1974) was a graduate of Cambridge University. He didn't take up golf until after his time at university but quickly became a scratch golfer. He worked as a golf club secretary for a number of years before turning his attention to golf course design. His career started after the Second World War when he assisted in the reconstruction of a number of war damaged course but he soon moved on to produce some original designs. He worked on some well known courses and helped to redesign Hexham, Northamptonshire County, Royal Lytham & St Annes, Saunton East, Sunningdale Old and West Lancashire.

More details about the move to the present clubhouse in the 1960s can be found in a later chapter.

1994 – The Blue course

Many of us remember the creation of the Blue course, designed by the local golf course architect, Simon Gidman. To facilitate a convenient start on either the first or last nine hole loop of the new course, required significant changes to the opening holes of the Red course. In fact, the first four holes of that course were completely replaced at the same time that the new 18-hole course was constructed.

Simon Gidman was an assistant professional at Gerrard's Cross Golf Club in the 1970's.

fourth tee - Blue course

He went on to study golf course architecture at Leeds Polytechnic being awarded a BA in 1982. He has worked as a golf course architect ever since.

The future

In 1908, the founders had the foresight to set up the Golf Club and a wonderful 18-hole golf course. Through the efforts of those who have followed, at the end of our first century, the Club has three fine 18-hole courses. Frilford is one of only a small number of clubs in Europe that can boast such a facility. One wonders where we will be in 2108 when the history of the second 100 years is written.

Fire at Frilford Heath Golf Club on Sunday 26 June 1921

The members of the Club were in for a huge shock when they turned up to play golf on the morning of Sunday 26 June 1921 as the following article in the The Oxford Times of 1 July explains.

The club house, professional's showroom and workshop and cycle sheds of the Frilford Heath Golf Club were completely destroyed by a fire in the early hours of Sunday morning. The club house, the walls of which were built of wood and the roof of thatch, was soon a wreck, and all that remains standing now are two of the chimney stacks. At present the cause of the fire is unknown, but it apparently occurred during the storm which raged over the country about one o'clock on Sunday morning. The assistant secretary Mr E. J. Jones and his son, who live at the Dog House close by, were the first to see the fire and endeavoured to call assistance by telephone from the Dog House, but the phone was out of order. It was impossible to check the fire in any way and the destruction was complete in half an hour. The professional's showroom and workshop, also the two cycle sheds, situated a few yards away, built of wood with galvanised iron roofs, shared a like fate and collapsed in quick succession. The smouldering wood was raked away as much as possible, but throughout Sunday and Monday frequently broke into flames.

The number of clubs and balls must run into thousands for in addition to the professional's stock most of the members kept their clubs and balls in lockers at the club house, while many had coats and shoes there as well. The assistant secretary and his son, Mr M. Jones when they

from the Oxford Journal Illustrated - "all that remains today"

first discovered the fire, made an endeavour, at considerable risk, to rescue some articles from the house, but beyond a few papers in the front house they found it impossible to get anything out. Lounge chairs and other club furniture, two garden seats, a cash register, two telephones and the contents of the refreshment store were completely destroyed.

The club house although unpretentious, provided considerable accommodation for the members, as, besides the clubroom, there were a ladies' clubroom, committee room, dressing rooms and lavatories. The professional's showroom and workshop were added about 1914 and the cycle sheds later.

The damage is estimated at between £4,000 and £5,000 which, we understand is, at any rate to some extent, covered by insurance.

The professional, Mr J. H. Turner, had been away playing in the Open Championship, and only reached Frilford on Sunday. He deserves special sympathy in that

he has lost, in addition to valuable stock, many things which cannot be replaced, such as photos, drawings and records in connection with his work as a golf architect. With commendable promptitude he got down from London new clubs, balls, etc., to supply members by Monday night.

The committee of the club had a hut erected for members, and hope in the course of a few days to get other huts up as temporary substitutes for a club house.

The Directors and Committee were quick to act. A special meeting of the Directors was convened at The Square House, Abingdon on 28 June. At that meeting, the Chairman, Claude Rippon, reported that the hut recently erected for the ground staff on the course had been moved and erected as a temporary shelter and that the Coach House at the Dog House had been fitted as a temporary workshop and that the professional had purchased a new stock of clubs, balls, bags etc.

The Mayoress of Abingdon and others at the official opening of the new clubhouse

The clubhouse - 1955

"One result of the weekend storm was that a City Dairy had 85 gallons of milk go sour. The owners were not pleased".

A subcommittee was formed and was given power *'to make such temporary arrangements as they should consider advisable and to consider places for erection of a permanent clubhouse and report to the Committee.'*

By the time of the next Committee meeting on 27 July 1921 it was reported that the subcommittee had purchased four temporary huts at a cost of £66 10s. With Mr J. R. Wilkins, architect, in attendance they also decided that they would not consider *'anything in the way of an elaborate clubhouse but only such as would give reasonable accommodation for the estimated probable future membership.'*

Mr Wilkins submitted elevations, plans and an estimate of cost – *'this being £5000 or by certain reductions £4500'.* The Committee approved this and agreed to send a circular letter to all members stating that nothing would be done without a meeting of the shareholders of the Company but that *'they were invited to intimate what support they would give to an issue of debentures – say for £20–£50 or £100 – to provide the necessary amount estimated at about £3500.'*

The next meeting was held on 1 September 1921, when the plans of the clubhouse were considered and the opinions of various members were sought as to the style and questions of future management. It was recorded that *'the only point the Committee have to deal with being the question of catering.*

It was clear that if the Club were to do all their catering the proposed plans would be useless apart from which anything in the way of full catering did not appear likely to be profitable.'

This meeting was followed immediately by a special general meeting, attended by 41 members, at which the plans for the new clubhouse were approved. At a joint meeting of the Committee and the Directors it was resolved that the tender from Messrs Woolridge and Simpson for the erection of the new clubhouse for the amount of £3089, be approved.

On 15 October 1921 the Committee appointed a House Furnishing Committee to consult with the architect as to the furnishing of the new clubhouse.

It was clear from the minutes of the Committee meeting held on 3 December 1921 that the new clubhouse was nearing completion because it was *'resolved that the Annual General Meeting (for 1922) be held at the new clubhouse on 15 December at 3 o'clock and that the House be formally opened on that day at 2.30 and that the Mayoress of Abingdon be invited to open it.'*

The formal opening was reported in The Oxford Times on 16 December 1921. It was a great achievement by all of those involved that the Club was fully operational in its new facilities within 6 months of the fire.

E J Jones

The minutes of 2nd June 1926 recorded:

"The Chairman stated that Mr E J Jones would shortly be retiring and the Directors had decided to grant him a pension and that it had been decided also to extend the courtesy of the club to him with the privliges of an ordinary member".

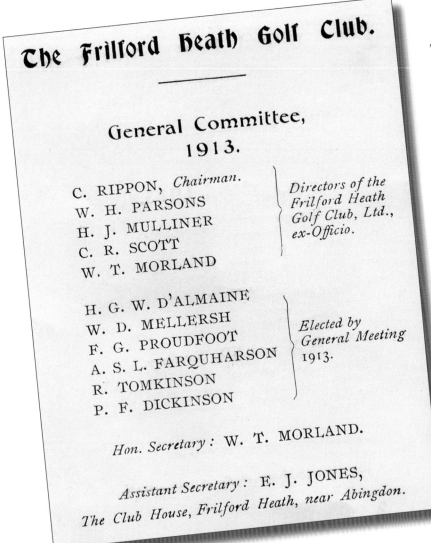

The minutes of 7th June 1947 recorded:

"The Chairman referred to the death of Mr E J Jones, who had been Assistant Secretary of the Club from 1913 to 1926. During this time he devoted his energies to the welfare of the club with efficiency and tact and his services during the clubs early years and his strenuous work during the 1914-1918 war had much to do with the clubs success."

The Amateurs of Oxford University

For many years there were arrangements for the University golfers to play at Frilford Heath on special terms. The University members were only in the area for perhaps 30 weeks of the year, returning home to various parts of the country when term was down. This was reflected in the reduced subscription paid by undergraduates. These arrangements were reviewed from time to time as is evidenced by the committee minutes of 5 June 1920.

The University also played a number of matches at Frilford Heath, evidenced by the minute of 15 October 1921.

Two students who came to Oxford in 1920 were to play together regularly and became two of the best Amateurs of all time. The golfers were Cyril Tolley and Roger Wethered. They both had remarkably similar golfing careers.

Cyril Tolley

Cyril Tolley was born in 1895. Awarded the MC during service in the Royal Tank Corps for leading his tank on foot during the battle of Cambrai, and taken prisoner in November 1917 he was 24 when he came to Oxford. He was already an accomplished golfer and was renowned to be a very long hitter of the ball. In 1920 he entered The Amateur Championship, held that year at Muirfield. He made it through to the final where he met a more experienced American, Robert Gardner. Tolley was not expected to win the 36 hole final. He did however triumph, beating Gardner on the first play off hole. The achievement didn't go unnoticed at Frilford Heath and on 24 July 1920 Cyril Tolley was conferred honorary status. Tolley went on to win The Amateur Championship again in 1929 when the matches were played at Royal St Georges. In the final he beat John Nelson Smith by a margin of 4 & 3.

He also won The French Open twice and six times played in The Walker Cup. In 1946 he was Captain of the Oxford & Cambridge Golfing Society. He won the President's Putter in 1938, also being runner up in 1921, 1923 and 1929. In 1948 he was Captain of the Royal & Ancient.

Roger Wethered

Roger was another fine amateur golfer. He entered The Open in 1921 while still an undergraduate, when it was held at St Andrews. Roger is remembered as one of those golfers who have arguably thrown away the chance to win in frustrating circumstances. In the final round on the 14th green, he was so intent on studying the line of his putt, that he stood on his ball!! Well, after the inevitable penalty was added to his score, Roger tied with Jock Hutchinson, an American. The rules at the time required a 36 hole play off. Apparently Roger Wethered needed some persuading to stay on in Scotland for the play off. He was due to play an important cricket match the next day that he didn't want to miss. He was persuaded and in the final scored 159 to Hutchinson's 150, to be runner up.

Roger Wethered too was conferred honorary membership.

The Varsity Match of 1920: the Oxford team included Roger Wethered (centre) and Cyril Tolley (right). On the left is R. R. Burton.

5. November 1921

invited Mr. R. H. Wethered to become an Honorary Life Member in recognition of his great effort in this years Open Championship.

A letter from him accepting & thanking the Club was read and one from the President of the O.U.G.C in appreciation of the Clubs action.

C. Rippon.
3/12/21.

Roger Wethered performed well in match play events, and played in The Amateur Championship on a number of occasions. In 1923 the championship was held at Royal Cinque Ports. Wethered beat Drew in a quarter final and was to play the winner of F Ouimet vs. C Tolley in another quarter final. In the event he didn't play his friend Tolley as he had lost to Ouimet. Wethered made it through to the final and he comfortably beat Robert Harris 7 & 6 in the 36 hole final. He was runner up in The Amateur twice and he played in the Walker Cup five times.

In 1948 he was Captain of the Oxford & Cambridge Golfing Society. He won the President's Putter in successive years twice, 1927 and 1928 and also in 1935 and 1936. He was also runner up in 1933 and 1949.

He was Captain of the Royal & Ancient in 1946.

Considered the stars of a new generation of golfers following the Great War and repeatedly bracketed together when comparing achievements, they were also good friends.

Both men played their part in the career of the legendary Robert T. Jones, 'Bobby Jones' who played against them in many Championship and Walker Cup matches.

Tolly's most famous match was a defeat. Defending his amateur champions title at St Andrews in 1930, he was beaten by Jones when he stymied himself and lost at the nineteenth, a match acknowledged by Jones, to have been one of his hardest ever. Jones progressed to beat Weathered in the final enabling him to go on and complete his famous 'grand slam'.

The three had much in common; university educated, resolutely amateur, they epitimised the glamourous sporting social elite of the 1930's. Roger's sister Joyce winner of five successive English women's championships in the 1920's was hailed by Jones as the best golfer, man or woman, he had ever seen.

Bobby Jones, Glena Collett and Cyril Tolly, Opening the Pasatiempo Golf Course, Santa Cruz, California 1929.
Julian P. Graham Historical Photographic Collection.

The 1931 Ryder Cup trial

There were two unofficial matches between Great Britain and the United States before the first official Ryder Cup match, which took place in 1927. The early games were played in 1921 at Gleneagles and then in 1926 at Wentworth. Samuel Ryder, the seed merchant from St Albans, brought the matches to the golfing calendar. He was in the bar after the matches at Wentworth and is reported to have said, "We must do this again". He donated the well-known gold trophy with a golfer on the lid, and the next match was arranged soon after that.

The first official match was played in the USA at Worcester, Massachusetts, over two days in June 1927. The format of the matches was almost as it is today, namely foursomes and singles. The matches were all played over two days. The USA won the series 9.5 to 2.5.

Two years later, in May 1929, the matches were played in Great Britain, at Moortown near Leeds. The British team fared better on home soil winning 7 to 5.

In 1931 it was the turn of the United States to host the matches. A few months prior to the match, trials were held in the same format as the actual matches, namely singles match play along the lines of a 'possibles vs. probables' game. The second trial was held at Frilford Heath Golf Club on Thursday 5 March 1931.

From Oxford Mail Wednesday 4 March 1931

Ryder Cup Trial

Arrangements for tomorrow's test at Frilford Heath

The second trial of the 24 Ryder Cup golf team nominees, which takes place at Frilford Heath tomorrow, will consist of two series of games at 12-a-side, the matches to be over 18 holes in each case.

H C Jolly (Foxgrove) is indisposed, and will be unable to take part. His place will be taken by Tom Green (Copt Heath), the Midlands professional champion, who was not included in the 24 players originally invited to hold themselves in readiness for the international match.

Play starts in the morning at 9:30, and in the afternoon at 2:00. Special buses are being run from Oxford at 9:30 and 1:30 (1s 6d return).

FAMOUS GOLFERS AT FRILFORD.

Mail

5TH

HURSDAY, 5 MARCH, 1931.

PRICE ONE PENN

ENCE CAMPAIGN CAL

RYDER CUP TRIAL AT FRILFORD HEATH

R.A. Whitcomb driving off from the first tee at Frilford Heath today in the Ryder Cup trial.
His opponent A.J. Lacy, is on the right.

On 7 March 1931, F H Taylor, the golf professional to the Oxford University Golf Club, wrote an article for the Oxford Mail. This reported on the match and also commented on a number of other interesting issues, not least of which was the use of the new sized, larger and lighter golf ball.

From Oxford Mail Saturday 7 March 1931

Reflections on Ryder Cup Trial

Encouraging form of Younger British Professionals

Effect of the lighter ball

By F H Taylor (professional to the Oxford University Golf Club)

In days past, Oxford, considering its size, has had more than its fair share of golf exhibitions. These have been due largely to amateur sides coming down to play the University, and it was not until four years ago that J H Taylor's team of professionals began their series of annual visits.

Nothing in the past , however, has been comparable in importance, interest, or instruction with this week's staging at Frilford Heath of the British Ryder Cup Trial match.

All visitors, both players and spectators, were loud in their praises of the excellent arrangements made for their comfort, and were impressed by the general excellence of the course.

The roping off of Nos 1 and 10 tees, was a sound scheme, for it allowed the players plenty of room and added to the comfort of the spectators. The white lines around the greens proved most valuable, and lessened the duties of the stewards in keeping the course clear. The arrangements for the referees and stewards were admirably carried out by Mr N F Henderson and Captain Borgnis, and, in fact, everyone connected with the organisation deserves high praise.

Captain Wickham had an anxious day, but the success of the meeting must have amply rewarded him. The excellent condition of the course was a worthy tribute to the work of the greenkeeper – Mr. Prickett – and his staff.

A Worthy Substitute

Owing to the sudden illness of the Ryder Cup Captain, Charles Whitcombe – the Frilford Heath professional, J H Turner, was called in to fill the vacancy, and that he did right worthily, only losing by one hole to S A Easterbrook in the morning, and winning by one hole from W H Davies, the Wallasey professional, one of our leading players, in the afternoon.

The combination of a fully stretched course, and the new larger and lighter ball made Frilford a good test of the game. The behaviour of this new ball was a great source of interest. It was pretty obvious that when well hit the loss in length was negligible. To say one loses 25 yards is a poor attempt to explain away a slightly miss-hit shot.

The most interesting thing to me was the difference in the way the short holes were played as compared with the way they undoubtedly would have been with the smaller and heavier ball.

Effect of the wind

The direction of the wind was down from the second hole, which meant coming from the right front at No. 5, dead against at No. 7, behind and slightly from the right at No.13 and across at No. 15. The play to No. 5 was fairly ordinary, except that wooden clubs had to be used, but at No. 7, which measures 164 yards, the results were very interesting.

When the players played the type of shot they would normally do, the breeze seemed to lift the ball higher, and helped the slight left to right spin to take the ball either into the bunkers on the right, or further wide, whilst those players who took a straighter faced club to knock the ball down, under the wind, found the green, though it was usually on the left hand side.

A little more practice would, I feel sure, have given these latter players a much greater reward for their skill, and rightly so, for skill and tactics should be more worthy of a good result than a mere hearty slap in a given direction, trusting to the weight of the ball to keep its line.

Another interesting point about the play to this hole was that when a player was wide of the green, he not infrequently got down with a chip and one putt, whilst perhaps more often, when a players tee shot was on the green, he took three putts.

The tee shots at No. 13 were hit, in my opinion, somewhat timidly, and so were regularly short and slightly cut, the player obviously feeling that the wind would take the ball right up to the pin, and forgetting that the lighter ball would not run like the heavier one.

The only hole on the course that was not reached in two shots was No. 16, which was dead against the wind, but even here Pagham was within eight or ten yards in the afternoon. (Editors note: this hole is the present 12th on the Red course).

Without doubt this lighter ball requires a greater measure of accuracy in those shots up to the hole, and I was particularly interested to hear from two or three players that they consider playing with the larger, lighter ball materially assists the U.S.A. players to maintain an ascendancy.

Putting Difficulties

However, at Frilford, most of the players seemed to have greater difficulty in putting than anything else. The greens were of a nice colour, even texture, and running fast, but I feel that with more grass there would have been fewer putts.

The meeting was a great success from every point of view, and should have imparted knowledge to many of the onlookers. The most pleasing feature to anyone who has the future of British golf at heart was the good showing of the younger players. Such players as A H Padgham and W J Branch will surely go far, and these games are of incalculable benefit to them in providing experience.

The only hole on the course to come in for any adverse comment was No. 18 where the back tee, the light ball and head wind made it almost impossible to reach the fairway, proving that a short two shot hole is the most difficult of any length to make good under all conditions. (Editors note: this hole is the present 14th on the Red course).

Professional golfers and members of the club gathered before the Trial matches.

The results of the Trials were as follows:-

Manager's team		Chairman's team	
Morning			
J H Turner	0	S A Easterbrook (1 up)	1
A Compston	½	A H Padgham	½
A Mitchell (2 & 1)	1	W J Branch	0
F Robson	0	H Large (2 up)	1
G Duncan(3 & 2)	1	W Large	0
P H Rodgers (2 & 1)	1	B Hodson	0
W H Davies (2 & 1)	1	Gus Faulkner	0
T Green (3 &1)	1	L Holland	0
D McCulloch (1 up)	1	W T Twine	0
E R Whitcombe	0	O Sanderson (5 &4)	1
R A Whitcombe	0	A J Lacy (2 up)	1
T Barber (2 & 1)	1	A Hewers	0
Afternoon			
Turner (1 up)	1	Davies	0
Compston (1 up)	1	Branch	0
Mitchell (3 & 2)	1	Padgham	0
Robson	0	Faulkner (5 & 4)	1
E Whitcombe	0	Duncan (5 & 4)	1
Rodgers	0	Lacey (1 up)	1
R Whitcombe	½	Havers	½
Green	0	H Large (4 & 3)	1
McCullock	0	Hodson (4 &2)	1
Easterbrook (3 & 2)	1	W Large	0
Barber	½	Holland	½
Twine	0	Sanderson (2 &1)	1

The 1931 Ryder Cup matches were played at Scotio in Columbus, Ohio over 26 and 27 June 1931. The matches were won by the United States, which won the first day's foursomes by 3 matches to 1 and the second day's singles by 6 matches to 2, an overall win of 9 to 3.

Charles Whitcombe was the playing Captain of the Great Britain and Ireland team and the players making up the team were:

Archie Compston
Fred Robson
William Davies
Abe Mitchell
Charles Whitcombe
Bert Hodson
Ernest Whitcombe
Arthur Havers
George Duncan
Syd Easterbrook

There are some interesting omissions from this 1931 British side. The rules of the competition, at the time, stipulated that a player had to be born in the country he represented and had to be resident in the country at the time of the matches. The best British player of the time was surely Henry Cotton but he was resident overseas. Another great player was Percy Alliss who was attached to a golf club in Berlin in 1931. He returned to Britain and being eligible again, played in the 1933 matches.

The British side sailed for the USA from Southampton on the RMS Majestic. Cotton and Alliss also travelled with the group and reported on the matches for the press. Peter Alliss has certainly followed in his father's footsteps in more ways than one.

In 1939, Players, the cigarette manufacturers produced a set of 25 cards called Golf. The series depicted famous professionals of the era each giving instructional tips. Reproduced below are three of the set, depicting A H Padgham, W H Davies and Syd Easterbrook.

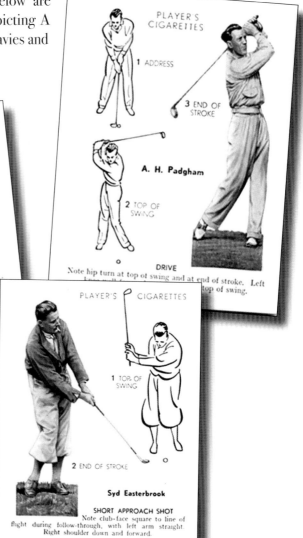

Royal patronage

If you have seen the letter from King Edward VIII hanging in the clubhouse, you are probably wondering why the Club is not referred to as 'Royal' in its title. Edward VIII certainly must have been delighted with the regular golf that he played at Frilford Heath if he was inspired to write this letter. But for a golf club to have the title Royal in its name is quite a different matter.

The fact that we have a letter from Buckingham Palace confirming that King Edward VIII bestows his patronage on the Club was indeed a great honour at the time.

We need to go back to basics though and have a look at the dictionary definitions of a couple of words.

Patron A patron is *'one who countenances, protects, or gives **influential** support to a person group or cause'*. In many ways all members of the club would consider themselves to be patrons of Frilford Heath Golf Club. But the important word in this definition is in bold. A patron is someone of real influence who lends support.

Patronage To show patronage is to show *'encouragement or support'*.

The fact that Edward VIII felt compelled to write this letter "bestowing patronage on the club" surely indicates that he was more than just an occasional member of the Club, that he felt an affinity for the Club and was happy to be associated with it.

A committee minute from 10th April 1915 states:-

"It was resolved that it be recorded that H R H The Prince of Wales, a frequent visitor of the Course, had requested the Club to invite subscriptions from Members towards the National Relief Fund and that as a result a sum of about £60 had been collected."

He was made an honorary member in 1921. The Annual General Meeting minutes of 15th January 1921 state:-

"Since the last meeting HRH The Prince of Wales has, in response to the Directors' invitation, graciously consented to become an Honorary Life Member, and following last year's Amateur Championship Meeting, the Amateur Champion Mr CJH Tolley had accepted a similar invitation."

Royal clubs have come about in a variety of ways. An authoritative book on the subject is Royal Golf, which was produced by Sir Peter Allen and published in 1989 by Stanley Paul & Co Ltd. This book tells the story of many of the Royals and how they came to be referred to in this way. In some cases clubs were Royal from the day they were incorporated. An example is the Royal West Norfolk at Brancaster, presumably because the then Prince of Wales in 1892 was a founder member and considered it to be very much his club.

Frilford Heath was not King Edward VIII's only golf club membership. He was also a member at The Berkshire when he was Prince of Wales. Some are surprised that The Berkshire Club never joined the band of Royals, given that the King was a member and that it is situated on Crown land close to Windsor Great Park.

The Crown Commissioners even paid for the construction of the course. The Berkshire was more likely to be conferred Royal status than Frilford Heath, but the Prince of Wales was upset by a particular incident with the Secretary of the club. It is alleged that the Prince was rebuked for bringing a golf Professional into the clubhouse for a drink. Archie Compston was a great friend of the Prince and they often played golf together. At that time though, Professionals were considered servants and were rarely allowed into the clubhouse. In the eyes of the Secretary at The Berkshire, bringing a Professional into the clubhouse must have been on a par with, for example, a scruffy tee-shirt or torn denims now!

Whether this anecdote is true or has been elaborated over time is not known. However, the Prince started to play more at Mid Surrey Golf Club and Royal status was conferred on this club in 1936.

Perhaps we will never know quite how close Frilford Heath Golf Club came to being known as RFHGC.

PRIVY PURSE OFFICE,
BUCKINGHAM PALACE, S.W.

30th March 1936.

Dear Sir,

I am commanded by The King to inform you that His Majesty has been graciously pleased to grant his Patronage to the Frilford Heath Golf Club.

Yours truly,

Wigram

Keeper of the Privy Purse.

The Captain,
Frilford Heath Golf Club,
nr. Oxford.

The stymie

To be stymied, is a term that has become fairly common in the English language. Most golfers are aware that a stymie is an old golfing term, but how many know exactly what it means?

Pat Minns gave me an old Frilford Heath score card from the 1930s, which incorporates a stymie measure on the back. I determined to find out precisely what it was used for.

Basically, in match play one had to play the ball as it lay, and if your opponent's ball was on your line, that was just too bad! What options did you have if you were 'laid a stymie' by your opponent. Well, firstly you could try to play around your opponent's ball, perhaps using the slope or borrow of the green to attempt to get your ball around the obstacle to just drop into the hole. A second option would be to take your mashie (modern day equivalent would be say an 8 iron), even though you lay on the green you would then chip the ball over your opponent's, perhaps leaving it stone dead by the hole, or better still, holing out the chip. This must have been a green keeper's nightmare. A lot of damage must have been caused to greens by inexperienced golfers attempting to negotiate the stymie.

In medal or stroke play, the stymie rule was not played. As is the case now, a ball would be lifted on the green if it were on the opponent's line.

A scorecard from the 1930's

Strokes	In Singles three-fourths of difference between handicap allowances. In foursomes three-eights of difference between the aggregate handicap allowances on either side. A half-stroke or over shall count as one. Smaller fractions count as 0.	Diff. in Handicap	Stroke Allow. Single	F'some
	< ·········· **STYMIE**			
	Frilford Heath Golf Club.			
1	12 PLEASE	1	1	0
2	2 12	2	2	1
3	2 6 12 REPLACE	3	2	1
4	2 6 12 14	4	3	2
5	2 4 6 12 14 DIVOTS.	5	4	2
6	2 4 6 10 12 14	6	5	2
7	2 4 6 8 10 12 14	7	5	3
8	2 4 6 8 10 12 14 17	8	6	3
9	2 4 6 8 10 11 12 14 17	9	7	3
10	1 2 4 6 8 10 11 12 14 17	10	8	4
11	1 2 4 6 8 10 11 12 14 16 17	11	8	4
12	1 2 4 6 7 8 10 11 12 14 16 17	12	9	5
13	1 2 4 6 7 8 10 11 12 13 14 16 17	13	10	5
14	1 2 4 5 6 7 8 10 11 12 13 14 16 17	14	11	5
15	1 2 4 5 6 7 8 10 11 12 13 14 16 17 18	15	11	6
16	1 2 4 5 6 7 8 9 10 11 12 13 14 16 17 18	16	12	6
17	All except 15	17	13	6
18	A stroke a hole.	18	14	7

MEASURE ·········· >

Frilford Heath Golf Club.
LOCAL RULES.

1. Balls are out of bounds when played over the fence on the left going to the 1st, 13th, 14th and 18th greens; also when over the fence beyond the 9th green. Balls are out of bounds and irrecoverable when played over the fence on the left going to the 2nd, 3rd, 4th, 16th and 17th greens.

2. Recognized Water Hazards are "Blackwater Brook," and cut Trenches thereto and the Ponds to the right of the 9th green.

3. The footpath crossing the course at the 5th, 12th, 14th, and 15th holes shall be deemed to be not a "hazard."

4. Balls lying within one club's length of any wall or boundary fence, or in Gorse, Bushes or Trees, (but not in long grass or heather) may be lifted and dropped under penalty of one stroke.

5. A ball lying on a putting green other than that of the hole which is being played MUST be lifted and dropped, without penalty, not nearer the hole.

6. A ball lying in a rabbit scrape or rabbit hole may be lifted and dropped not nearer to the hole without penalty. If in a hazard it must be dropped in the hazard.

7. When a ball is lifted and dropped under Local Rules (except under Rule 5) the player shall keep the place from which the ball is lifted as nearly as possible between himself and the hole.

8. A ball lying within 20 yds. of the pin, except in a hazard, may be lifted and cleaned, provided that the position of the ball be first located in the angle of a club and replaced exactly in the original position. A penalty of one stroke if a ball be lifted without first marking the position with a club.

9. If any player's handicap should be altered during the progress of a competition, this alteration does not effect his handicap for the remainder of this Competition.

10. Players in a Competition shall be entitled on request to pass Non-Competitors.

11. A full round may be commenced at the 1st or 10th Tee at option. Matches which have played nine holes shall be entitled, on arrival at the 10th or 1st Tee, as the case may be, to follow immediately after one new match of those already waiting on those respective tees.

12. A ball lying in a cart rut or in the track between cart ruts may be lifted and dropped not nearer to the hole without penalty.

As is so often the case even now though, the rule in match play was quite different. I suppose the stymie was a direct result of the fact that in match play one is not playing for a score against the card but playing the opponent.

As you can imagine, a stymie could have a significant impact on the result for the hole. A hole that looked as if it might be won, could be lost if one were 'laid a stymie'. The player who was likely to lose the hole might try to putt his ball to a strategic point on his opponent's line; this being a better option than holing out.

Even in match play though, you didn't have to play the ball as it lay if it were too close to your opponent's. If it were within 6 inches, you could ask your opponent to mark and lift his ball. One can imagine the arguments that might ensue if there was not a measure available. Hence, clubs would often include the stymie measure on the score card. In fact, this is why many clubs produced score cards to exactly that width.

The stymie was abolished by the R&A in 1951.

Burrows good and bad

In the 1930s, the leading weekly golf magazine was Golf Illustrated. A regular feature article each week was entitled 'Burrows Good and Bad'. The writer of these articles remained anonymous because he toured the country to report on the condition of various golf courses. In the issue of 17 July 1937 it was the turn of Frilford Heath to face the scrutiny of 'Brer Rabbit'.

Some holes had been altered or extended since the course was originally laid out so the full text of the article is reproduced here, there are some interesting comments.

All the way from Maidenhead one is travelling through the loveliest countryside imaginable to find at Frilford Heath, the journey's end, close to Abingdon and near to Oxford; golf equally lovely.

There is about the Frilford Heath Golf Club an atmosphere, a personality, that I found quite charming and particularly attractive.

I sensed it the moment we drove into as spacious as complete, and as well arranged a car park as I have found for many a day. This car park and the clubhouse beyond, with its verandah gay and scented with hanging flowers, seemed fresh and clean and rain licked. It gave promise of a well organised club, where one's reception would be kind and courteous and where one's every want would be met, and it was a promise that was quickly and amply fulfilled.

I have spent many happy days golfing all over the world. I have never spent a happier one than the one I spent at Frilford Heath, and I look forward, as I have never looked forward more, to a return visit.

There are two courses at Frilford Heath, one of 18 holes and one of 9. I played the 18; I hope one day to play the 9,

Frilford Heath Golf Club.

MEMBER'S PASS.
(*Not Transferable*).

Available till 31st December, 1934.

Name *P Darby Esqr.*

R. F. E. WICKHAM,
Secretary.

No.

which, I was told, would provoke my interest and stimulate my golf. If it is at all like the 18 I played, it will.

The Frilford Heath course measures 6,306 yards and has a bogey of 74. Being heathland turf it is as dry as a bone and as soft to walk upon as any Ispahan. Prior to my visit it had been raining, which is to say that the fairways and greens were emerald in colour and true as a billiard table. I found too the bunkers well tended and the teeing grounds and their appointments well kept. This later to me, a small matter though it may be, is always a sign of exceptional industry and affection on the part of the green staff.

This course, which I would liken to Sherwood Forest, impressed me with the worth and variety of the second shots it demands. One can be hitting the ball exceptionally well from the teeing grounds, and Frilford Heath with all its fairways fringed with gorse insists upon good driving, and yet unless one is hitting the ball accurately with one's irons the sum total of one's strokes can mount to an appalling total. And this insistence on fine iron play is maintained throughout the eighteen holes. One is given no breathing space as I found to my discomfiture just when I was beginning to think that I was master of the situation.

Let us take some of these fine seconds.

We get one at the second (410 yards). Played over rising ground to a well trapped and well orientated green it has to be struck powerfully almost through the eye of a needle.

Yet another comes at the third (458 yards). Here control as well as power and accuracy come into the picture. Ground falls and a fine collecting bunker on the left have to be taken into one's calculations.

Still another comes at the sixth (446 yards), a beautiful dog-leg hole to the right, where with the second it is so easy to be a little too much to the right.

So far we have had long seconds. Two of a shorter variety come at the eighth (332 yards) and the ninth (350 yards). Both greens are defended by hollows of considerable depths which have been fashioned into hazards. Both these seconds are deceptive to a degree, especially the one at the ninth, and they will repay the deepest consideration and a precautionary stroll forward.

At the tenth (411 yards) we get another long second which has to be steered home with the ground and past flanking bunker.

The twelfth (477 yards) presents a grand second over and past a veritable nest of trouble. A great hole this twelfth since it requires in addition to that grand second a powerful and well placed drive. It is so easy to be just wrong.

The fourteenth (437 yards), a beautiful hole, provides yet another lovely second, as does the sixteenth (469 yards). This latter hole, with an out of bounds on the left and a series of hazards on the right, demands a long tee shot placed slightly to the left of the fairway and then leaves one with a second to be worked in through a bottle neck.

The seventeenth (371 yards) and the eighteenth (338 yards) offer two short seconds, the seventeenth a high flung pitch to a bowl green and the eighteenth a hummocky run up. But the strength of both these holes lies with the tee shot, the seventeenth a sharp dog-leg to the left, in particular a demanding shot that must have about it not only power and accuracy but courage. As one views the prospect from the teeing ground one is inclined to become obsessed with the coward's way well to the right.

I did not like the short holes at Frilford Heath except the excellent fourth (298 yards) which, strictly speaking is not a short hole at all. But Frilford Heath remains in my mind a charming course.

Hole.	Yards.	Bogey.	Strokes.	Score.	Result.
1	367	4	10	-	—
2	410	5	2	6	o
3	458	5	17	5	o
4	298	4	5	4	o
5	198	3	14	4	—
6	446	5	3	5	+
7	164	3	12	3	o
8	332	4	7	4	+
9	350	4	16	6	—
	3023	37			

Name of Player **P. R. Darby** Hcp. **12** Date **1st Dec 1932**

Hole.	Yards.	Bogey.	Strokes.	Score.	Result.
10	411	5	6	5	+
11	486	5	9	6	o
12	477	5	1	5	+
13	178	3	13	1	+
14	427	5	4	6	o
15	126	3	18	3	o
16	469	5	11	5	o
17	371	4	8	4	+
18	338	4	15	4	o
	3283	39			

BOGEY PLAY.

Holes won ....

Holes lost ....

Result

If hole is won put +

" " " halved " O

" " " lost " —

MEDAL PLAY.

Gross Score ....

Handicap ....

Net Score

Marker's Sig. **a. Victor Franklin**

Author's notes

References made 70 years ago by Brer Rabbit to many of the holes could have been written only yesterday. A cross reference to the holes as they are played today is set out below.

1937	2007
2nd	15th Green course
3rd	lost hole, but the green now 8th Red course
6th	lost hole, but the green now 1st Green course
8th	3rd Green course
9th	4th Green course
10th	15th Red course
12th	lost hole, but the green now 6th Red course
14th	lost hole
16th	12th Red course (but green was further back into the woods)
17th	13th Red course
18th	14th Red course

Mr. P. Holmes with his caddy   84

Frilford House
The purchase of Frilford Heath House in the 1960s and the creation of the 36 holes

By the mid 1950s, golf generally had recovered from the effects of the Second World War and by 1959 membership of Frilford Heath Golf Club had reached pre-war levels at 379 men and 125 ladies. Each year between 70 and 90 new members were admitted; a net gain of about 20. Television and Great Britain's victory in the 1957 Ryder Cup played significant roles in bringing golf to the attention of the sporting public and by 1963 full playing membership had risen to 630.

Visitors to Frilford Heath Golf Club were plentiful; for example, Friday, 14 September 1962 saw 73 visitors, whilst there were 57 on the following Sunday. In 1963 there were twelve societies playing over weekends (paying green fees of £1356). Discussion as to the control of visitors and societies continued to occupy the attention of the Committee and the Directors found it necessary to remind the Committee that applicants for membership were expected to be experienced golfers with an existing handicap at another club. A waiting list did not exist in those days, exclusivity was required but not at any cost. The 1960s saw a steady rise in membership and the Directors considered that urgent action was necessary to avoid congestion on the courses. In consultation with the Committee a theoretical maximum membership was to be agreed in

line with existing numbers and not exceeded. Visiting societies would only be permitted on week days. In the event, however, membership declined and the Committee noted in 1970 that it no longer considered congestion on the courses to be an issue (they were premature, there was a waiting list with 400 names on it by the end of the 1980s).

Against this background, Frilford Heath House and its adjoining 44 acres, immediately adjacent to the 3rd and 4th holes of the old course came onto the market. The owner, Archibald Thornton West had died some years earlier and the property was sold by his executors. It was a substantial country estate that even included a well maintained cricket pitch played on by a local village club. The property commanded some interest, not least from the then Captain of the Club who eventually offered the asking price of £18,500, which was hastily withdrawn when he was advised that the Company was also bidding

This Conveyance

is made the Eleventh day of May — One thousand nine hundred and sixty-three BETWEEN AUBREY WILLIAM SCHUSTER of Number 4 Copthall Court in the City of London Stockbroker PETER EDWARD FRANCIS ARCHIBALD WEST of The Coutt Axbridge in the County of Somerset Electrical Engineer and HENRY EDMUND SARGANT of Number 10 Little College Street in the City of Westminster Solicitor (hereinafter called "the Vendors") of the one part and THE FRILFORD HEATH GOLF CLUB LIMITED whose registered office is at Boswell House Broad Street in the City of Oxford (hereinafter called "the Purchaser") of the other part

W H E R E A S :-

(1) Archibald Thornton West late of Frilford Heath House in the Parish of Marcham in the County of Berks a Major (retired) in Her Majesty's Army (hereinafter called "the Testator") died on the Twentieth day of October One thousand nine hundred and fifty two and Probate of his Will was granted to the Vendors out of the Principal Probate Registry on the First day of January next following.

(2) The Testator was at the date of his death seised of the property hereinafter described for an estate in fee simple in possession subject as

1964 purchase of Frilford House from the estate of A T West

for the property and offering the asking price. The minutes of the Directors' meeting records that the Company had agreed to purchase Frilford Heath House 'with the intention that the facilities should be extended to two 18 hole courses in order to make provision for the ever increasing number of applicants for membership who may be expected now and in the future'. The Committee heard the announcement 'with great satisfaction'.

The Company now found itself facing a dilemma. It's resources were sufficient to complete the purchase of Frilford Heath House and bank finance was available to cover the cost of the course alterations and the construction of the new holes but would not extend to the provision of a new clubhouse. Nevertheless, the Company pushed ahead with the appointment of course architects to design the new layout and work commenced in the spring of 1964 to the designs produced by C K Cotton & Partners, but with the question of funding for a new clubhouse being left in the air.

Members were divided on the proposals submitted: to adapt Frilford Heath House by no means an ideal building; update and improve the existing clubhouse; or build anew. However, the members were becoming impatient and the Directors instructed the architects to prepare schemes both for the conversion of Frilford Heath House and the

updating of the existing building. It being generally agreed that a new building, however desirable, would be too expensive and would entail the demolition of Frilford Heath House as no other suitable site was apparent.

The Chairman made it clear at the 1965 Annual General Meeting that the company's financial position did not permit the Directors to proceed with the construction of a new clubhouse. However, he said he very much looked forward to the day when the club would be leaving the present building, with its ever increasing noise from traffic, which might be in 7 to 10 years time. In the meantime, construction of the new courses was completed and formally opened in September 1965.

The Company announced that if the conversion of Frilford Heath House into a new clubhouse was to proceed they expected support from the members. They proposed a members' loan scheme, whereby for each £100 lent, the

member's subscription would be reduced by 5 guineas. The proposal did not find favour with the members and, although the company had secured planning permission for the conversion of the clubhouse, it was considered necessary to defer seeking tenders for the building work. Nevertheless, the project had gained momentum and an 'off-the-record' meeting took place in December 1967 between four long-standing members. The members were represented by the Captain, Dr Bill Reynard (Chief Medical Officer for the Pressed Steel Fisher Company) and Ray Ellis, much respected Regional Manager of National Provincial Bank and Captain elect. The Directors were represented by Norman Challenor, a local solicitor and coroner, and John Pether, whose family had been connected with the Company for many years.

It was readily agreed by these members that there was no substantive reason why the necessary funds should not be forthcoming.

The Clubhouse - 1972

A 1960's view of the 9th green Red course, with the thatched cottage in view beyond.

*4th October 1969 -
the new clubhouse is
officially opened for
business*

It was decided that Ray Ellis, following his appointment as Deputy Captain at the forthcoming 1968 Annual General Meeting, would explain some fine tuning that had been suggested with regard to the repayment of the members' loans and that a letter would be circulated to the members encouraging them to support the Company. The initial response promised sums in excess of £37,000 so the Company was able to invite tenders for the building work in October 1968.

Architects for the project were Harry W Smith and Son of Osney Mead, Oxford, and the main contractor for the project was Upper Reaches Construction Limited of Abingdon. The new clubhouse was formally opened a year later, in November 1969. The former country house was already substantial and certainly larger than the former pavilion by the Dog House crossroads. The internal alterations together with the modern extension provided a dining room to seat 100, a mixed bar to accommodate 150, a men's bar, a ladies lounge, a committee room, a steward's flat, a professional's shop and generous parking. These were a significant improvement on the facilities available at the former clubhouse. The total cost of the works was £100,000, of which the member's loans had contributed £41,000. The member's loans were repaid over the coming years and completely repaid in the early 1970's.

Three years later, the site of the old clubhouse was sold to Berkshire County Council allowing it to stagger the crossroads. While the Chairman and members were able to enjoy the peace and quiet afforded by the new clubhouse some years earlier than predicted without the members' support.

G R D Eyles

G R D Eyles was born on 27 June 1953. He joined Frilford Heath at the age of 10 having previously benefited from 6 years on the practice ground. Dickie lived adjacent to the Course which, in those days, comprised 27 holes. His house was adjacent to the 18th tee on the Red Course (now the 14th).

His first taste of golf was in 1957 when he was taken on to the Course at the age of 4 by his Grandfather, Cyril Viney. 18 years later, Dickie went on to become the most successful golfer produced by Frilford Heath.

At the age of 11, he had a handicap of 20 and was often called upon by the then Secretary, Jack Acres, to represent the Club in inter-club matches. By the age of 13, he had acquired a handicap of 4 and won a scholarship to Milford School in Somerset.

The handicap system in those days was vastly different to the current system and you had to have full international status to become a + category player. When the Frilford clubhouse was being moved to the current site, Dickie held the composite course record, at the age of 13, with a gross 69.

At the age of 21, Dickie held five amateur course records, which included a 67 at Burnham Beeches and a 65 the following day on the Green Course at Frilford Heath in the Club Championship. He also held the record with a 65 at Burnham and Berrow.

He played in his first Open Championship at Troon as an amateur in 1973, having pre-qualified at Glasgow Gailes with rounds of 73 and 70.

The Open was won that year by Tom Weiskoff, Dickie failed to make the cut with rounds of 86 and 76. The first round was played in a gale, the results reflecting the difficult weather conditions with the best score being a 69 by Gay Brewer.

Internationals 1973-1975

Dickie continued to progress and he achieved his first International honour in 1973, representing England Youth. He represented England Youth in 1973 and 1974, British Youth in 1974 and achieved full international status that year playing for England at Royal St Davids.

Dickie continued to impress and, in all, represented England 15 times, winning eight, halving one and losing six of his international fixtures. He also represented England in the St Andrews Trophy in Italy in 1974, and Great Britain in the Eisenhower Trophy in La Romana, Dominican Republic in the same year. This was won by America with Great Britain in sixth place.

Top row: P J Hedges, H B Stuart, Dr D M Marsh (non playing captain), C W Green, J Davies, I C Hutcheon.
Front row: M A Poxon, G MacGregor, G R C Eyles, M James, P Mulcare.

Walker Cup Team
1975 at St Andrews

Walker Cup 1975

Dickie's finest achievement was to receive Walker Cup honours in 1975 when he was selected to represent Great Britain and Ireland against the Americans at St Andrews.

The media, at the time, commented that, as often in the past, the results proved that the most effective performers on the British side were those playing for the first time. Mark James, the then English Amateur Champion, Dickie Eyles, Ian Hutcheen and Pat Mulcare all had their moments of glory. When an unfortunate accident prevented Peter Hedges from playing on the first day, Mark James found himself called into both opening matches paired with Dickie. They were successful in the foursomes on both occasions, with Dickie hitting the opening drive in the tournament.

One of the commentators said that he could not recall any British pair playing with greater composure in their first match.

Dickie's results in the match were:

Won I UP   R D Eyles & M James
              v   J Pate & R L Siderowf

Lost 2 & I   R D Eyles
              v   J Haas

Won 5 & 3   R D Eyles & M James
              v   W Cambell & J Grace

Lost 2 & I   R D Eyles
              v   W Cambell

Professional

Dickie turned professional in 1976, playing on the European Tour until 1980. The format for Tour events then comprised a pre-qualifying round on the Monday. The first two rounds proper were played on Wednesday and Thursday. Then, after the cut, came the last two rounds of the tournament. Any player who had made the cut to play in all four rounds of the competition gained exemption from playing in the qualifying round for the following week's tournament.

Dickie returned to playing at Frilford Heath in 1983 as an amateur, where he is held in high esteem by the members and, while not often on the course these days, he will offer advice and experience when requested. He is still able to perform to a high standard.

1975 - Captain Norman Holmes on behalf of the members presents a gold watch to Dickie Eyles in recognition of his gaining a place in the Walker Cup team

Myles Boddington

Myles Alan Boddington was born on 30 November 1924 in Cheshire. He went to school at Rugby where he followed in his father's footsteps and excelled at cricket. He captained the school in his final year and played for the Royal Air Force against Worcestershire.

Myles lived in Burford for most of his life. He joined Frilford Heath in 1962 and was also a long time member of Burford Golf Club. He was a fine golfer (a left hander), who won the club championship at both of these clubs. He was also a very accomplished administrator, particularly when it came to golf.

Myles served the Berkshire Buckinghamshire and Oxfordshire Union of Golf Clubs for many years and was President of the Union for a three year term, from 1972 to 1974.

He was a member of the R&A, golf's governing body, and served on a number of its committees. He chaired both the amateur status and the championship committees.

Myles was also President of the English Golf Union, the governing body for men's golf in England, in 1978.

England v France 1984 and 2008

Frilford Heath Golf Club has been fortunate and proud to have hosted a number of important amateur golf tournaments. One such tournament, which came to the Club in 1984, was the amateur International match between England and France.

The game between England and France was first played in 1934. Initially, the match was played annually, alternating between England and France. The matches were not played during the war years but were revived in 1947. From 1950 onwards the matches became biennial affairs, but they ceased after 1962. Apparently it was decided that the match had no real benefit because England invariably won!

Mr K K Smith, President of the English Golf Union, set the wheels in motion to revive the matches and they recommenced in 1982 with a match in Chantilly, France. In 1984 the matches were played at Frilford Heath and the Club presented a silver salver, which is still played for. The salver was presented to the then Presidents of the English Golf Union

Dallas Stevens presents the new salver to the Presidents of the English and French golfing unions

The 1984 England side who played against France at Frilford Heath

(Douglas E Johns) and Federation Francaise de Golf (Richard Rahusen). The Chairman of Frilford Heath, Dallas Stevens, made the presentations and can be seen in the centre of the photograph marking the occasion.

The match at Frilford Heath consisted of four foursomes matches in the morning and eight singles in the afternoon, on both Friday 20 April and Saturday 21 April.

For the French, the most notable member of the team was Jean Van De Velde. He may have been new to international competition, being just 17 years old at the time. He only competed in the Saturday singles and won his match comfortably 6 up with 4 to play.

For the English, the well known amateur, Peter McEvoy played in all four matches, securing 2 ½ points out of a possible 4. Another player who is well known to many in this area is David Lane of Goring & Streatley. He is still a top amateur, and now plays in Seniors matches. He still plays off a very low handicap and was recently President of the Berkshire Buckinghamshire and Oxfordshire Union of Golf Clubs. David did not play in the foursomes but did play in each day's singles; winning both of his matches.

The overall result was England 16 France 8.

Frilford Heath Golf Club is proud to have been asked to host the match again in the centenary year. The matches will be held over the weekend of 10/11 May 2008. Members would be well advised to watch as much of the golf as they can. There are sure to be some great golf matches and who knows, you could be watching future Walker Cup players, future top professionals or even major championship winners to be. And despite the inevitable outcome in the 1930s and 1940s, don't be fooled into thinking that the result will be a forgone conclusion. Since 1994, France has won as many times as England; this should be a close match.

Peter MvEvoy

The development of the Blue course

How instructive it would be if we could be transported back in time to talk with the great golf course architects of over 100 years ago. To speak with the likes of J H Taylor and James Braid, to ask them what was in their minds as they thought out some of their great courses from the bare land they were presented with. What an insight that would give us of the courses that we now play over.

Well, in another 100 year's time when our successors are celebrating 200 years of golf at Frilford Heath, they will not have to speculate about the formation of the Blue course. The architect, Simon Gidman has written the following passage for us. Now that the course is over 10 years old and well established, members can reflect on the intentions and challenges set for them.

By Simon Gidman

With social activities taking a far higher priority than architectural matters during the Christmas period and contractors always on holiday for two weeks, I tend to follow suit and take two weeks off during the Christmas break. However, for reasons I can't remember, I decided to work over the Christmas period of 1993 and much to my surprise received two good enquiries. One was a call from the then secretary/manager of Frilford Heath Golf Club, Jacques Kleynhans, asking me, along with five other architects, to tender for the design of the new Blue course. The odds of 1 in 6 were not good, but the Club is very local to me and it would have been a tremendous feather in the cap to be awarded the contract.

So on the premise of 'nothing ventured nothing gained', Nick Blakemore (my partner at the time) and I attended an interview in early January and discussed the project with the board of Directors headed by the Chairman, Mr Skelton, with Jacques Kleynhans in attendance. It was explained to us that pressure on the existing Red and Green courses had led the Club to purchase the nearby farm, comprising about 170 acres. The intention was to retain the Red and Green courses for the benefit of the members and to offer the new Blue course for society use and to relieve the two main courses of excess play. As the new course would be intended primarily for society use, two loops of nine holes were essential, which in turn necessitated alterations to the existing Red Course.

We discussed the method of construction and were told that the Club was keen to keep costs in check. In principle, the architect was to undertake all the planning issues and prepare detailed plans and the Club would undertake all the construction works, root zone mixing and spreading, as well as all cultivation and irrigation work. In terms of construction, I had never known a golf club undertake so much and frankly I was concerned that carrying out all the work was a little beyond them.

I knew that the then Course Manager had undertaken quite a bit of construction work but even so, the construction of a complete golf course from start to finish is a major undertaking. Furthermore, I knew that one of the fundamentals of success was to have an experienced machine driver, or 'shaper' as they are known in the construction industry. These people are the unsung heroes of golf

course construction. Good ones, speedily and carefully, shape the subsoil to the architect's plan adding all the little idiosyncrasies illustrated on the drawings that really bring the plans to life. Without a decent shaper, it doesn't matter how good the plans are, the golf course will never be as interesting as it should be. American architects tend to take their own shapers with them wherever they go, relying on local earthwork contractors to move the subsoil and relying on their shaper to do all the detailed work. I had seen inexperienced shapers at work before and did not like the results and I was not keen that, for such a prestigious new course, the earth shaping should be undertaken by anyone lacking the required experience.

The question was, as one of six selected architects, dare I jeopardise our chances by questioning the Club's approach to the construction method. However I wanted the Club to be fully aware of my views before selection so took the plunge. I cannot, in

all honesty remember their response, but I remember leaving the meeting with more than a slight doubt that my questioning of the method of construction had probably jeopardised our involvement.

Barely two weeks passed before we were asked to attend another meeting and were told that the Club liked our approach and that we had been awarded the contract. We were asked to progress with the planning application as quickly as possible. Back in the early 1990s, planning was a lot easier than it is now. There was no need for excessive survey work or Environmental Impact Assessments, which can take months to prepare and can be very costly. The number of plans required was also considerably less than needed now. However, the site had its own sensitivities in terms of wetland areas (beside the stream) and acid heathland (on the higher areas), which the Club had nourished and developed as part of the Red course. With these two sensitivities in mind, our main planning discussions were held with the Environmental Agency the name of the officer dealing with the plans was Heather Whetter! The bulk of the site was of little interest to the planning authorities and, apart from the careful rehousing of a badger sett, the planning went fairly smoothly.

After all my initial fears about the handling of the contract, the Club agreed with me on the need to employ specialised golf course contractors. From a tender list of five, John Greasley was nominated to undertake all the site clearance and earth movement works with the Club completing the drainage, cultivation, planting and irrigation works. Later, in 1997, the 10 million gallon irrigation lake was added to ensure that all the fairways and approaches were watered during the summer, thus maintaining the high expectations of the Blue course.

Starting and finishing points at holes 1, 9, 10 and 18 meant that some of the original holes on the Red course (holes 1, 2, 3 and 4) had to be redesigned and re-sited on the new land. 170 acres is ample land on which to build 18 to 22 holes but it did mean that the holes from the Red course had to be rehoused on what was fairly dull land. The existing Red and Green courses have a considerable charm of their own, part of this derived from the interesting land form, which can, to some extent, be reproduced by machine shaping, but also owing to the general landscaping and development of woodland, heather and gorse, which takes more time.

The routing of the Blue course took on a fairly strict orientation. With the need to have two loops of nine holes on the Blue course as well as including four new holes for the Red course (which had to be physically separated from the Blue course) the holes took on a fairly rigid east to west arrangement. We tried, wherever possible, to counter this with holes running in a more north to south route and we achieved this with holes 1, 2, 5, 6, 7, 13 and 16, but most holes run in an east to west direction. Still, if it works at St Andrews...

Furthermore, the new Blue course needed to have a character of its own. New courses need to create an immediate impact, so architects

plan major changes in levels to create an interesting and immediate landscape. Because the original site was so flat, this modern approach would work well at Frilford Heath and

A minor problem during construction and new machinery ready for use as the course opens

by about 1 metre, partly to take the holes out of the flood plain and partly to be able to shed surface water to positive outfall points. Forming levels to shed surface water away from greens and off fairways is the mantra of most golf course architects but in this case the fall across the site was barely 4 metres from the central pine woodland to the stream, so this was another difficulty to surmount. The sub base was relatively sandy and would therefore drain well, but architects tend to ignore this fact and rely more on a positive movement of water across the site to a stream or ditch.

At a more detailed level the new Blue course needed to be of a different design from the Red and Green courses. Putting surfaces were designed to be larger and more rolling with specific pin areas designed for competition and easier pin positions for everyday play. Equally, to allow for more play, the teeing grounds were made correspondingly larger and bunkers, or to be more precise bunker numbers, were increased with more elaborate designs. I am a great believer, at least on new sites, of clusters of three or four smaller bunkers designed together, rather than the American approach of large sandy wastes. Throughout the course there are groups of bunkers, sometimes merging with bunkers on other holes (e.g. holes 11 and 17), which form quite a tight grouping of sand features.

I have always been a great fan of Shinnecock Hills Golf Club on the eastern seaboard of America and in particular the positioning and scale of the bunkers there. At Shinnecock, the bunkers are not particularly glamorous to look at but they are perfectly to scale and match the broadness of the landscape. They also direct

would help to create a degree of individuality to the course that would separate it from the Red and Green courses. On the question of earth shaping, I loathe the idea of forming lumps either side of a flat fairway and calling it a 'links' course. For the new design to work well, the fairways and rough areas had to be regraded so that the whole site worked as one rolling landscape. Furthermore, allowances had to be made for the four holes to the south of the site, bordering the stream, which were generally within the local flood plain. This area was very low lying and it needed to be raised

The Chairman of the company Joe Skelton and 1994 Captain Barry Mainstone officiate

golfers along a particular route, creating interesting fairway shapes and challenging the golfer to select the best route from tee to green classic strategic golf. I have tried to repeat some of the same principles on the Blue course. The design of hole 12 illustrates the point. I would not normally put in three or four bunkers alongside a fairway with the associated large mounding as on hole 12. However, the idea here was partly to break up the spaces between this hole and hole 17 and also to encourage the better player to get as far up (and into the narrowest part) of the fairway as possible to get both the best view and the shortest shot into the green.

One of the most difficult problems, particularly on a relatively dull site, is to come up with different challenges on each hole. The layout of the course was not too difficult, partly because of the space available, but also, rather oddly, because there was little of interest around which the course could be organised. The site was almost a blank canvas, which is, of course, a double edged benefit.

On such a site, the difficulty is to create interest and challenge in equal measure. As with the design of hole 12, I would not normally design bunkering quite like that on hole 7. I know that bunkers 30 yards or so short of a green are very annoying to golfers, particularly when there are no obvious features around the green itself to act as a distance indicator. But this was deliberate, and golfers on this hole are being asked to assess the yardage to the green and to be bold in the execution of the shot. This was a technique often employed by architects from a different era when they would place a bunker

104

well short of a green and make the land between the approach bunker and the green blind. The golfer would assume that the green started just beyond the bunker, which of course it did not, and the player would often be left exasperated, having hit what they thought was a good shot to the green only to be left 30 or so yards short. However, it takes a different form of precision to play this shot well. How dull would the course be if every fairway had a bunker located either side of the dog-leg point and each green a bunker either side of the putting surface?

Members assembled before the opening ceremony

I hope players will find the course well balanced in terms of difficulty. Many of the par 4s (even short holes like number 2) are quite hard holes and certainly holes 9 and 18 are very tight finishing holes where a bogey is not necessarily a poor reward. Balanced against that, the par 5 holes, 8 and 15, are relatively easy and one would hope to make birdies on both these holes as one would on hole 5. A good course has a mix of difficult and easy holes, some testing the drive, others the second or third shots and hopefully this balance and challenge have been created on the Blue course.

Water is not hugely significant on the course and in many ways it is not required. There is water entwined around holes 1 to 4 but this is only because the stream comes naturally into the layout on these holes. Stating that water comes into play on the first four holes does seem to contradict most philosophies of golf course architecture where an easy start is normally vital both for the speed of the round as well as the psychological well being of the golfer. Despite the fact that hole 2 is short, holes 1 to 4 are difficult, certainly harder than holes 10 to 14 and I often wonder whether the two nines should not be reversed to reflect this.

Now, some 10 years after its construction, I still enjoy returning to the course, seeing the landscape evolve and the condition constantly improve. I hope that the golfers do not curse the architect too much after the first two holes, but see him in a different light having picked up birdies at the easier par 5 holes.

Major competitions at Frilford Heath

Research indicates that from its formation 100 years ago, the Club has recognised the importance of competitive golf at a high level.

Clause (g) of the Articles of Association drawn up when the club became a limited company states an objective of the company is *to promote and hold competitions and matches in connection with golf and to contribute to prizes, medals, cups, testimonials and other rewards and to arrange and pay for exhibition matches and competitions between professionals and to promote, give or support luncheons, dinners, concerts and other entertainments.*

The arranging of exhibition matches was a primary objective and these matches were organised between the very best golfers of the day. The match to celebrate the official opening of the course in 1909 is reported earlier in the book. It was played between two of the very best British golfers of the day, Harry Vardon and J H Taylor. The fee required by the players is not known but would have been a significant sum. However, times change and it is no wonder that such matches are not a part of the calendar today. Imagine what it might cost to bring say Nick Faldo and Colin Montgomerie to Frilford Heath for a day now! The world of professional golf has of course changed immeasurably in the last 100 years. Back then, the top professional would make his living from such exhibition matches, playing in hundreds of them a year up and down the country. There were serious competitions such as The Open to be played in, but these bought little reward, even to the winner. Our own Professional, J H Turner, played in The Open Championship in 1921. The minutes of the Committee meeting of 2 April of that year record:

It was resolved that the Secretary be authorised to post a subscription list inviting members to contribute towards the Professional's expenses in connection with the Open Championship competitions.

There were further exhibition matches after the First World War.

From the minutes of 1919:

The Secretary reported that A Mitchell, G Duncan, J G Sherlock and J H Turner had been booked to play on 6 May 1919.

And then in 1920:

The Chairman reported that an Exhibition Match had been arranged to take place on 11 November 1920, J H Taylor & J H Turner against C J H Tolley & R H Wethered, the professionals giving their services (except Taylor's travelling expenses), admittance to the course 2s/6d (including tax) the proceeds to be given to the Radcliffe Infirmary, Oxford.

This match predates the formation of the National Health Service by a good few decades, so this is a precursor to a modern day charity golf day. In those days, funds were raised by charging spectators to watch top professionals rather than levying a fee to play the course as happens today.

J H Tolley and R H Wethered were at Oxford University and J H Turner was the Frilford Heath Professional. J H Taylor was certainly very generous on the occasion of this charity event.

In the 1930s the club hosted the Ryder Cup Trials, which are reported earlier in the book.

Such matches appear to have fallen out of the golfing calendar at Frilford Heath in the 1930s, perhaps the financial difficulties the country faced were a significant factor.

A more recent way of bringing together professional and amateur golfers is the 'Pro Am'. The format is usually a four ball game in which a professional plays with three amateurs. Pro-Ams are played regularly on the day before European Tour events and they are also regularly arranged at Frilford Heath; indeed they are one of the highlights of the calendar. Presently, the professionals playing in the Frilford Heath Pro-Am are all club professionals from the Berkshire Buckinghamshire and Oxfordshire Professional Golfers Association; places are keenly applied for.

In 1974, the Thomas Cook International Pro-Am Golf Tournament was held at Frilford Heath, in aid of Save the Children. Back in the 1970s it was still possible to attract top professional golfers to local events, as can be seen from the list of golfers playing in May 1974.

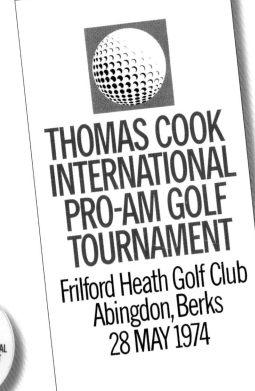

SOME OF THE PLAYERS

PETER ALLISS. Though not a regular tournament player, is still one of the best strikers of a golf ball in Britain. Now better known as a journalist, commentator and golf course architect.

HUGH BAIOCCHI. South African, 1973 Swiss Open Champion, and third in the PGA Order of Merit.

BRIAN BARNES. One of the tours longest hitters. Member of the last three Ryder Cup teams, and fifth in the Order of Merit.

MAURICE BEMBRIDGE. Regarded as Britain's most travelled golfer. Second in the Order of Merit and winner of Martini Tournament in 1973. Former Dunlop Masters and PGA Champion.

NEIL COLES. Winner in 1973 of Spanish Open, the Benson & Hedges Matchplay Championship and the Sumrie Clothes Better-Ball (with Bernard Hunt). Runner up in the British Open with a last round of 66. Seven consecutive appearances in the Ryder Cup.

BERNARD GALLACHER. Three Ryder Cup appearances before he was 25! One of the most consistent players on the circuit.

BRIAN HUGGETT. Winner of many championships since 1962, the latest, the Portuguese Open last month. Five appearances in Ryder Cup matches and the only unbeaten player in the 1973 series.

BERNARD HUNT. Consistent winner of tournaments since 1953. 1973 British Ryder Cup Captain and eight times a member of the team.

DAVID JAGGER. Probably the most improved young golfer of 1973, moving to 24th in the Order of Merit. Winner of the 1974 Kenya Open.

CHRISTY O'CONNOR. Irelands favourite and most famous golfer. He has the unique record of ten consecutive appearances in Ryder Cup matches. Winner of most of the major British titles, except the 'Open'.

PETER OOSTERHUIS. First in the Order of Merit for 1973, for the third year running – a record in itself. Winner of the 1973 Piccadilly Medal, French Open and Viyella PGA Championship.

EDDIE POLLAND. Most improved player in 1973. Finished sixth in Order of Merit and gaining a Ryder Cup place. Best British player in the World Cup – 7th place.

DAI REES. Many times member and captain of the Ryder Cup team. Has won every major British title except the 'Open' in which he was 2nd on three occasions.

PETER TOWNSEND. Despite having a moderate year, by his own high standards, has the ability to be a front runner for 1974 honours. Was joint individual winner of recent Britain v Japan match.

THOMAS COOK INTERNATIONAL
PRO-AM GOLF TOURNAMENT
Frilford Heath Golf Club,
28 May 1974
MEMBER

THOMAS COOK INTERNATIONAL PRO-AM GOLF TOURNAMENT

Frilford Heath Golf Club
Abingdon, Berks
28 MAY 1974

10p

In aid of The Save the Children Fund

TIME	PROFESSIONAL AND AMATEUR PLAYERS						
08.15	**G. Legouix**	G. R. D. Eyles	(Scr)	J. D. Skelton	(6)	N. J. Holmes	(11)
08.24	**D. Vaughan**	C. Brooks	(8)	A. W. C. Thurgood	(8)	D. Eke	(10)
08.33	**P. Butler**	C. Westerman	(18)	J Stewart	(2)	R. Alexander	(14)
08.42	**M. Gregson**	J. M. Brice	(18)	A. J. Pett	(14)	J. Frith	(10)
08.51	**N. Hunt**	J. Doyle	(18)	M. Rodgers	(16)	B. Woods	(15)
09.00	**B. Hutchinson**	G. Broadbridge	(16)	Col. Lincoln	(12)	K. Fujita	(18)
09.09	**D. Rees**	D. Wildsmith	(17)	J. Luxon	(18)	A. Corbett	(7)
09.18	**G. Cunningham**	D. R. Bailey	(5)	Capt. Brounger	(13)	C. Dixon	(18)
09.27	**N. Wood**	D. Boe	(18)	Brig. Davenport	(6)	L. Owen	(11)
09.36	**N. Job**	A. J. Taylor	(7)	P. Trower	(7)	G. Swann	(18)
09.45	**G. Will**	J. Russell	(17)	K. Musto	(14)	P. R. Knowles	(13)
09.54	**J. Garner**	P. Ryan	(16)	T. Husbands	(14)	D. Vidler	(6)
10.03	**V. Baker**	D. Nixon	(18)	E. P. Gibson	(9)	I. Gallop	(12)
10.12	**C. DeFoy**	J. Baker	(9)	M. Wates	(18)	F. R. Williams	(12)
10.21	**B. Huggett**	S. Kimmins	(12)	J. A. Bailey	(18)	J. S. Hasselwood	(11)
10.30	**W. Humphreys**	M. Wells	(7)	R. Bromley	(16)	A. Hitchcock	(13)
10.39	**D. Jagger**	J. Mullarkey	(14)	R. Rodney	(12)	R. W. Windle	(11)
10.48	**H. Jackson**	C. G. Stow	(15)	I. Scott	(9)	G. L. Bradbury	(18)
10.57	**B. Hunt**	A. Anderson	(5)	P. Wilmoth	(18)	R. E. Burrows	(12)
11.06	**P. Wilcock**	R. D. A. Galbraith	(18)	R. Hayes	(18)	W. M. Guthrie	(15)
11.15	**D. McClelland**	G. E. Powderham	(18)	B. Heirs	(14)	J. Cooper	(18)
11.24	**H. Muscroft**	J. Diggle	(5)	B. Lakey	(18)	W. G. Seabrook	(12)
11.33	**C. O'Connor**	J. F. McGiven	(16)	T. J. Eames	(12)	P. Merttins	(9)
11.42	**J. O'Leary**	M. Wilson	(11)	R. Betts	(10)	P. Lagden	(16)
11.51	**P. Alliss**	B. Amos	(14)	N. A. Campbell	(15)	J. Gillum	(7)
12.00	**B. Gallacher**	H. T. K. Haslam	(18)	J. Cookson	(9)	P. Soper	(18)
12.09	**E. Polland**	W. Craft	(12)	Dr. Crawford	(6)	J. Byron	(12)
12.18	**T. Horton**	J. C. Boxall	(18)	G. Peel	(8)	A. R. Cole-Hamilton	(4)
12.27	**N. Coles**	P. F. Gardiner-Hill	(5)	D. Jenkins	(18)	J. M. Townsend	(12)
12.36	**B. Barnes**	R. Tucker	(13)	D. A. Sack	(12)	R. Tindale	(9)
12.45	**H. Baiocchi**	L. Rawlings	(6)	J. Stokes	(7)	J. A. Lee	(14)
12.54	**M. Bembridge**	P. Dobereiner	(11)	J. F. Whitfield	(8)	J. Cox	(14)
13.03	**C. Clark**	Air Commdr. Wright	(10)	D. R. L. Wallace	(9)	F. C. Batstone	(18)
13.12	**P. Townsend**	E. G. Thomson	(9)	T. Graveney	(7)	R. C. Fairburn	(6)
13.21	**P. Oosterhuis**	D. G. Barber	(3)	E. W. Swanton	(13)	S. Roberts	(9)

The match details are correct at the time of going to press; any late amendments will be published immediately prior to the event.

What of top golf at Frilford Heath at the turn of our first century? Well, the Club does not seek to hold top professional events, such as European Tour events because they would be far too disruptive to the members and costly to stage. However, the Club is proud to take its turn in hosting major amateur events, whenever asked to do so. A summary of the national amateur events held over the last 25 years follows.

1973 – County Finals (ELGA)

The four leading county scratch teams play in the finals over three days. Foursomes is played in the morning and singles in the afternoon, with each team playing each other over the three days.
Played over the Red course.
Winners – Northumberland, runners up – Warwickshire.

1984 – England v France (EGU)

This International match is the subject of a chapter elsewhere in the book.

1987 – English Amateur Championship (EGU)

Handicap limit - 2
Maximum number of competitors - 288
2 rounds of stroke play, 64 lowest scores and ties play in match play knock out thereafter over 18 holes with the final being played over 36 holes. The competition was played over a composite course comprising the first 9 holes of the Red course, followed by holes 1 to 4 and then 14 to 18 on the Green course, This was a tough test indeed, being over 6500 yards and a par of only 71.
K J Weeks beat R Eggo in the final on the 37th hole.

1989 – County Finals (ELGA)

The four leading county scratch teams play in the finals over three days. Foursomes is played in the morning and singles in the afternoon, with each team playing each other over the three days.
Played over the Red course.
Winners – Cheshire, runners up – Essex.

1992 – Ladies' British Open Amateur Stroke Play Championship (LGU)

Handicap limit – 6
Maximum number of competitors – 120
72 holes stroke play. 36 holes played on the first and second days.
40 players returning the lowest scores and ties play a further 36 holes on the third day.
Winner Miss J Hockley (287), runner up Miss R Bolas (290)

1996 – English Champion Club Tournament (EGU)

Each County Union has a competition to decide their champion club. This competition brings together a team of three players from each of the champion clubs. All three players play 36 holes of stroke play with all three medal scores counting. The lowest scratch score is the winner.
The winning club represent England in the

European Champion Club Tournament. The championship was played over the Blue course and was won by Hartlepool Golf Club (Durham County Union) with a score of 287.

1997 – Senior Ladies' British Open Amateur Championship (LGU)

Handicap limit – 9
Maximum number of players 90
Players to be aged over 50 on the first day of the championship.
54 holes stroke play. 36 holes played on the

first and second days.
40 players returning the lowest scores and ties play a further 18 holes on the third day.
Winner Mrs T Weisner (231), runner up Miss V Hassett (236).

1999 – The Seniors Open Amateur Championship (R & A)

This championship was first played in 1969 and now attracts a very wide international field.
Handicap limit – 5
Maximum number of competitors – 252
Players to be aged over 55 on the first day of the

1992 -Ladies British Open Amateur Stroke Play Tournament

championship.

54 holes stroke play. 36 holes played on the first and second days. 60 players returning the lowest scores and ties play a further 18 holes on the third day. The competition was played over the Red and Blue courses.

Winner Bill Shean Jr. from Hinsdale, Illinois (219)

2000 – English Ladies' Open Mid-Amateur Championship (ELGA)

Handicap limit – 9
Maximum number of competitors – 60
Players are to be aged between 18 and 50 on the first day of the championship.
2 rounds of stroke play, 32 lowest scores and ties play in match play knock out over 18 holes. Played on the Red course.

Winner Miss K Keogh (Crompton & Royton Golf Club) beat Miss R Prout in the final.

2003 – English Seniors Championship (EGU)

Handicap limit – 12
Maximum number of competitors – 240
Players to be aged over 55 on the first day of the championship
54 holes stroke play. 18 holes played on each of the first and second days on two different courses. The 60 players returning the lowest scores and ties play a further 18 holes on the third day. Played over the Red and Blue courses.

Winner D Arnold (218)

2006 – Ladies Home International Matches (LGU)

The matches comprise amateur teams of 6 players, from each of the four home nations, England, Scotland, Wales and Ireland. Over the three days each team will play the other three teams, playing foursomes in the morning and singles in the afternoon.

Played on the Red course, England were the winners with 16.5 points, Ireland second with 14.

2007 – Ladies' British Open Mid-Amateur Championship (LGU)

Handicap limit – 9
Maximum number of competitors – 120
Players are to be aged over 25 on the first of January in the year of the championship.
3 rounds of stroke play with a cut for the top 40 players after the first two rounds.

Played on the Red course, the event was won by Emma Duggleby of England (Malton & Norton Golf Club) with a score of 220.

2008 – England v France (EGU)

To be played on the Red course in May of this year.

* Organised by:-

EGU	English Golf Union
ELGA	English Ladies Golf Association
LGU	Ladies Golf Union
R&A	Royal & Ancient

Major club trophies

Founders Bowl

This magnificent trophy was presented in 1926 by the founders of the club, H S Challenor, A E Preston and T Skurray. The inscription reads 'presented to the club by H S Challenor, A E Preston and T Skurray, the makers of the course'. This trophy was originally played for over two consecutive Saturdays as a 36-hole strokeplay competition under handicap. The first winner in 1926 was T Cotmore who also won the grand sum of £5.

In the second year of this competition it was decided that the competition should be held on one day and prizes given for the best morning and afternoon rounds. In 1951, the Founders Bowl was considered to be a possible trophy for the Club Championship, but the Morland Cup was chosen instead. The current 18-hole format was introduced in 1981.

J T Morland Cup

The J T Morland Cup was one of the original trophies played for at Frilford Heath and was first mentioned in the minutes of 1914. It was originally a medal competition played for twice a year in June and December. In the early days, entries for this competition were poor, so in 1924 the format was changed to a strokeplay competition under handicap. In 1951 it was agreed that the J T Morland Cup would be awarded to the winner of the Club Championship, as it still is today.

Cowley Cup

In 1921, Mrs M B Cowley presented a silver bowl to be played for annually in the autumn under the Calcutta Cup Scheme. The Calcutta Cup format was devised in 1885. It was originally a handicap tournament played for by holes won, shots being given by holes and not shots. In 1924 it was agreed that this trophy should be played for in the autumn under knockout conditions, pretty much as we play it today. For a short time in the mid-1930s the maximum handicap for this competition was 16, and it was played for as a bogey competition.

Harvey Cup

P G Harvey presented this Challenge Cup in 1927, to be played for under Jubilee Vase conditions. The Jubilee Vase came into existence as a competition in 1887. It was a handicap competition more akin to strokeplay than matchplay. In 1931 it was decided to change the format to ordinary matchplay rules, and in 1935 it was played for as a medal competition on the first Saturday in April. It is unclear when the competition changed to its current knockout format, but it was probably in the early 1940s.

Mellersh Cup

In 1915, Mrs Mellersh presented a silver cup in memory of her late husband, W D Mellersh, to be played for annually as close as possible to his birthday in May. The original cup was destroyed in the clubhouse fire of 1921, and was replaced by the current cup in 1924. Originally a matchplay competition, it has recently been played for in its current 18-hole bogey format.

Brownlow Cup

This cup was presented by the Hon M Brownlow in 1935. It is played for as an 18-hole qualifier; the top 16 going forward into the knockout stage under handicap.

Stradling Cup

In 1947, Arthur Stradling presented a silver trophy to be played for as a summer knockout competition. The Committee at the time decided that it should be used for the Club foursomes competition.

Veterans Cup

The Veterans Cup was presented by W T Morland in 1927. Whilst there is no early reference to the original qualifying age for this tournament, we do know that it was changed to 55 years in 1938. The age qualification was changed again in 1951 from 55 to 60 years and it was also decided that play be from the 'normal' rather than the 'competition' tees.

Knipe Bowls

These bowls were presented by Mr and Mrs JW Knipe in 1931. It was originally agreed that the bowls be played for on the first Thursday in October as a bogey competition with a maximum handicap of 18. This is a mixed foursomes competition.

Jack Acres Trophy

In 1982, it was decided that there should be a 36-hole medal event to be called the Acres Cup in recognition of the then Club Secretary, Jack Acres. The trophy was renamed the Jack Acres Trophy; the format remaining unchanged to the present day.

Presented to the
FRILFORD HEATH GOLF CLUB
by
J O SKELTON
on the opening of the
BLUE COURSE
1994

Skelton Salver

This salver was presented by the then Chairman, J O Skelton, in 1994, to commemorate the opening of the Blue course. The format is unchanged from its original 18-hole medal competition. The competition is played for on the Blue course, annually in July, as close as possible to the anniversary of its opening.

Dallas Stevens Cup

Originally known as the Winter Fensomes Competition, this trophy was presented in 1982 by the then Chairman, Dallas Stevens. This winter knockout competition is still known as the Dallas Stevens Cup.

North Berks Cup

There is some historical significance to this trophy. The North Berks Golf Club predates Frilford Heath Golf Club and was a close neighbour, playing on a course at Shippon. When Frilford Heath Golf Club was formed, a number of members joined from The North Berks Golf Club, which folded at a later date. This trophy was presented to the secretary of North Berks Golf Club and the inscription on the trophy reads -

TO C.ALFRED PRYCE

FROM THE MEMBERS OF THE NORTH BERKS GOLF CLUB IN GRATEFUL APPRECIATION OF THE MANY YEARS SERVICE GIVEN BY HIM AS HONORARY SECRETARY TO THE CLUB

XMAS DAY 1908

This trophy is played for by male members, the format being scratch knockout.

Mens Club Championship - J T Morland Cup

Year	Champion	Year	Champion	Year	Champion
1925	H A B Whitelocke	1959	J Coomber	1988	S Walker
1926	R W Langford	1960	J T Franklin	1989	M C Lewis
1927	C W Parry	1961	A H Busby	1990	T Wallis
1928	H S Burrough	1962	C A Uttley	1991	A C Parry
1929	G H Dulake	1963	J Coomber	1992	N Paterson
1930	A V Franklin	1964	J Coomber	1993	A Gavrilovic
1931	F G Proudfoot	1965	J Coomber	1994	D P King
1932	J M Taphouse	1966	J T Franklin	1995	L Jackson
1933	H S Burrough	1967	T O'Callaghan	1996	B Monks
1934	R Ellis	1968	J A Putt	1997	K Johnson
1935	R Ellis	1969	R A Coulson	1998	J Lawson
1936	F V Spiller	1970	M Boddington	1999	J Lawson
1937	F V Spiller	1971	J Coomber	2000	M Haddy
1938	J G Griffiths	1972	G G Benson	2001	P Bickerton
1939	R Cox	1973	R A Coulson	2002	A D Walton
1940 - 1946	Not played	1974	G R D Eyles	2003	A Gavrilovic
	during war years	1975	R J Ellis	2004	E Wise
1947	W H Taylor	1976	J Coomber	2005	Dr P Collier
1948	R G Parsons	1977	C J Bartholomew	2006	M Woodbridge
1949	C B Bowles	1978	C J Bartholomew	2007	E Pepperell
1950	W J Head	1979	R J Ellis		
1951	C B Booth	1980	J Coomber		
1952	R G Seaver	1981	J A Evans		
1953	C B Bowles	1982	A C Parry		
1954	D Stevens	1983	D H Webster		
1955	E J Pether	1984	J P Goodman		
1956	C B Bowles	1985	A C Parry		
1957	C B Booth	1986	A C Parry		
1958	J Coomber	1987	S Walker		

Ladies Trophies

Andrew Walsh Cup

Mrs Andrew Walsh presented this cup in 1930. It is a spring pairs competition with an 18-hole strokeplay qualifying round; the top eight qualifying for the knockout stages.

Scratch Cup Championship

Now known as the Club Championship, this competition was first played for in 1931. This is a 36-hole scratch medal qualifying competition played over the Red and Green courses. Since 1989, handicap prizes have also been awarded

President's Challenge Cup

This cup was presented by Mrs Hippisley in 1923. It was played for as a knockout matchplay competition under full handicap.

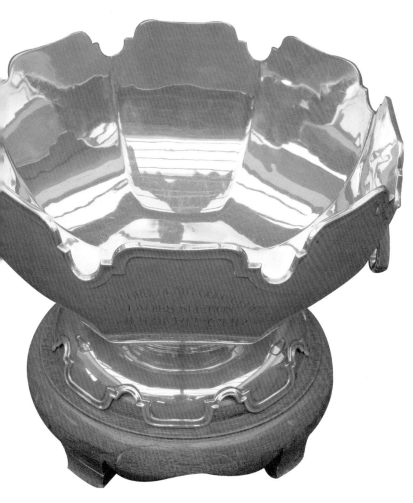

Jubilee Bowl

This bowl, donated by Lady Cowley was first played for in 1935 and was one of the original competitions played for in the Ladies Section. It is an 18-hole medal qualifying competition played for in the mid-summer to maximise entries.

Bronze Championship

The Bronze Championship was originally played for in 1948, and was formerly known as the Bronze Scratch Cup. This competition is only open to players in the Bronze Division. It is an 18-hole qualifying medal competition, played for on the same day as the Club Championship.

Coronation Salver

This salver was bought by the Club in 1953, and is an 18-hole medal qualifying competition.

Skelton Salver

This salver was presented by Mr and Mrs J O Skelton in 1994 to commemorate the opening of the Blue course. It is always played for over the Blue course on a date as close as possible to 1 August. It is an 18-hole qualifying medal competition

Millennium Crystals

This competition was introduced in 2000 by the then Lady Captain, Pam Matthews, to celebrate the millennium. These new, modern design, trophies are played for in a pairs competition over all the courses. It is a medal competition and the trophies are presented to the pair with the best combined net score from the three courses.

Ladies Club Championship - Scratch Cup

Year	Champion	Year	Champion	Year	Champion
1931	Mrs W J L Wallace	1964	Mrs J E Knott	1991	Miss L King
1932	Mrs C P Webber	1965	Mrs J E Knott	1992	Miss L King
1933	Mrs C P Webber	1966	Mrs J E Knott	1993	Miss L King
1934	Mrs R S Machin	1967	Mrs J E Knott	1994	Mrs J De V Hunt
1935	Miss D W Gradwell	1968	Mrs J G Glennie	1995	Mrs J De V Hunt
1936	Mrs T G Evers -	1969	Mrs J G Glennie	1996	Mrs M Huntley
	Mrs W H Margetis	1970	Mrs J G Glennie -	1997	Miss N Woolford
1937	Mrs T G Evers		Mrs M Huntley	1998	Miss S Huntley
1938	Mrs J D Edwards	1971	Mrs G Paulin	1999	Miss S Huntley
1939 - 1946	Not played	1972	Mrs J G Glennie	2000	Miss J Corkish
	during war years	1973	Miss P A Eyles	2001	Miss S Huntley
1947	Mrs C B Booth	1974	Miss P A Eyles	2002	Miss N Woolford
1948	Mrs N Trepte	1975	Mrs M Huntley	2003	Mrs S Webb
1949	Miss G Hawthorn	1976	Mrs M Huntley	2004	Mrs R Wilcock
1950	Miss C E Bowen	1977	Miss A Payne	2005	Mrs R Wilcock
1951	Mrs N Trepte	1978	Miss A Payne	2006	Miss J Binning
1952	Mrs J E Knott	1979	Mrs M Huntley	2007	Miss J Binning
1953	Mrs J E Knott -	1980	Miss A Payne		
	Miss B Benfield	1981	Mrs M Huntley		
1954	Mrs J E Knott	1982	Mrs J G Glennie		
1955	Miss B Benfield	1983	Miss L King		
1956	Mrs J E Knott	1984	Mrs B Wilenkin		
1957	Mrs J E Knott	1985	Mrs M Huntley		
1958	Mrs J E Knott	1986	Miss L King		
1959	Mrs S R Crawley	1987	Miss T Craik		
1960	Mrs R Wolfe	1988	Miss T Craik		
1961	Mrs J E Knott	1989	Mrs B Wilenkin		
1962	Mrs R G Seaver	1990	Miss L King -		
1963	Mrs R G Seaver		Mrs B Wilenkin		

The Ladies

The following notes have been researched from the minutes of the Ladies section of Frilford Heath Golf Club.

Ladies were first admitted to Frilford Heath Golf Club in 1913, when 19 lady members were accepted. At that time, there were no ladies tees and the first bogey was fixed at 86. A small committee was formed, and Mrs Hippisley became the first Ladies President. She remained in this post until after the Second World War.

At that time, the men's Committee decided what rules should apply to the ladies section. One of these rules was that ladies should give way to men on the course. Other rules were rigidly enforced, for example, two ladies played a knock-out final and stopped half way for lunch; they were made to replay the match without a break!

The First World War broke out in 1914 and nothing progressed until 1920 when play recommenced in earnest. After persistent lobbying for ladies tees, some were completed and Miss Bastin, a lady from the Ladies Golf Union, visited Frilford Heath and fixed the ladies par at 76 and the bogey at 79; handicaps were in the range 0 to 30.

After the disastrous fire at the thatched clubhouse, a new clubhouse opened in 1921. Soon after this, Oxford University, who had lost their course at Kennington, came to play at Frilford Heath. Some very good lady players were regulars at Frilford Heath, Joyce Wetherhead being one of them. Some matches were played during this time.

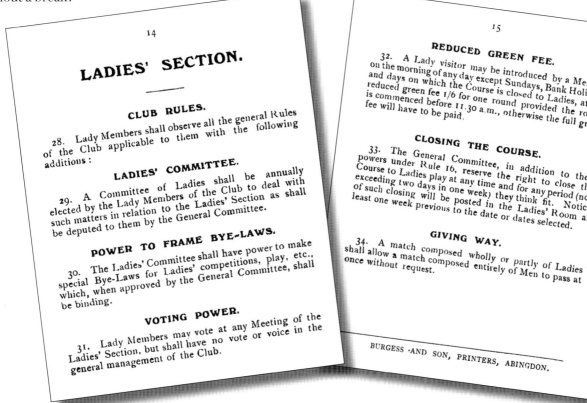

14

LADIES' SECTION.

CLUB RULES.

28. Lady Members shall observe all the general Rules of the Club applicable to them with the following additions :

LADIES' COMMITTEE.

29. A Committee of Ladies shall be annually elected by the Lady Members of the Club to deal with such matters in relation to the Ladies' Section as shall be deputed to them by the General Committee.

POWER TO FRAME BYE-LAWS.

30. The Ladies' Committee shall have power to make special Bye-Laws for Ladies' competitions, play, etc., which, when approved by the General Committee, shall be binding.

VOTING POWER.

31. Lady Members may vote at any Meeting of the Ladies' Section, but shall have no vote or voice in the general management of the Club.

15

REDUCED GREEN FEE.

32. A Lady visitor may be introduced by a Member on the morning of any day except Sundays, Bank Holidays and days on which the Course is closed to Ladies, at the reduced green fee 1/6 for one round provided the round is commenced before 11.30 a.m., otherwise the full green fee will have to be paid.

CLOSING THE COURSE.

33. The General Committee, in addition to their powers under Rule 16, reserve the right to close the Course to Ladies play at any time and for any period (not exceeding two days in one week) they think fit. Notice of such closing will be posted in the Ladies' Room at least one week previous to the date or dates selected.

GIVING WAY.

34. A match composed wholly or partly of Ladies shall allow a match composed entirely of Men to pass at once without request.

BURGESS AND SON, PRINTERS, ABINGDON.

The first ladies trophy was given in 1923 by Mrs Hippisley, and was known as The President's Cup. It was won for the first time by Mrs Pebody, who much later became the Ladies President. In 1924, the first Open Meeting was held and was considered to be a great success.

In 1927, two divisions were formed for medals and bogeys. Handicaps were 0 to 20 in the Silver Division and 21 to 36 in the Bronze; scratch for the course was 77. A request was made for ladies cards to be printed and this request was granted. There was a shortage of lower handicap players, and in 1928 a Bronze team was formed. In 1929, the membership rose to 179 and in 1930 a first team was formed and a first team tie was commissioned. This could only be bought from Walters in The Turl, Oxford, and only if a letter signed by the Lady Captain was produced! It was during this period that a charabanc was hired to transport the ladies to matches. In 1930, the handicaps were changed to 1 to 18 for Silver Division and 19 to 36 for Bronze Division. Also at that time, Mrs Andrew Walsh presented a trophy to be played for in a knock-out competition over 2 days.

In order to improve the ladies changing room facilities, one of the ladies asked if she could provide face powder and cream. This offer was gratefully accepted.

The Ladies Committee ran their own competitions but were still subject to the rules of the club made by the men. One lady was disqualified for playing in a competition with two men. During this period, subscriptions were 5 guineas for men and 4 guineas for ladies. Weekday green fees were 3/6d and weekend green fees were 7/6d. Mrs Belcher presented the ladies with a Scratch Cup to be played for at Closed Meetings.

In 1939 the country was once again at war, so no competitions were held and the Club was helped to carry on by willing older members. Some members did cycle to the Club in order to have a game. However, because of the transport difficulties in getting to Frilford Heath, a Ladies Committee Meeting in 1940 was held in the tea rooms of Elliston & Cavell in Oxford. At that meeting it was decided to organise a golf competition in aid of the Red Cross. This was open to non-members and the entrance fee was 3/6d, of which a minimum of 2/- was donated to the Red Cross.

In 1944 another Ladies Committee Meeting was again held in Oxford, this time at the Randolph Hotel. It was called to review the rules of the ladies section and the following additions were made:

1. Men were not to be allowed in the ladies changing rooms.

2. Dogs were not to be allowed on the course.

3. Meals were not to be taken in the ladies changing rooms.

4. Any alterations or additions to the ladies changing rooms, decided by the Men's Committee, must be referred to the Ladies Committee.

After the war everything got going again. There were 146 lady members, but many were non-playing members. There were 9 Silver players and 41 Bronze players. A letter was sent to the Men's Committee asking if they would give a donation to buy a prize for one of the ladies meetings. They kindly donated 5 guineas.

In 1949, Mrs Pebody became the Lady President. She was always impeccably dressed in velvet picture hats and swathed in furs. The Annual General Meetings she presided over were very dressy affairs. One lady appearing in a swans' down hat!

In 1950, Barbara Knott, the then Lady Captain, wanted to stage the County Championship at Frilford Heath. The Ladies Golf Union agreed to this and Barbara won the Championship. Betty Bowen joined the Club as a full member, having retired from work. Her handicap was 6. She proved to be a stalwart and influential member of the ladies section and, eventually was Lady President for many years.

In 1951, the Club sent a representative to London to vote in favour of the English Ladies Golf Association being formed.

It was in the early 1950s that the ladies asked if a footbath could be installed in the changing rooms. The reply was that a footbath could be installed if the ladies were prepared to give up one of the two toilets. Needless to say, this suggestion was turned down and the ladies settled for a jug and washbasin!

Qualifiers for the Andrew Walsh Cup - 1960's

In 1953, the Coronation Salver was purchased out of funds for £25 and played for in Division 1. Many more trophies were given over the years and are listed at the end of this chapter.

1963 saw the purchase of Frilford Heath House and more land. The house was converted into a new clubhouse and the additional land was used for the construction of the Green and Red courses, which were officially opened in 1969.

The 1970s were quiet years, but in 1973 the County Finals were held at Frilford Heath for the first time. 1976 was a very hot and dry summer with only two notable very wet days, Men's Captain's Day and the day the Coronation Foursomes Finals were held. 202 ladies competed, their handicaps ranging from single figures to 36. What with the torrential rain and the inexperience of the helpers, rounds took 5 hours to complete! For the first and only time, the thatched cottage (which stood between the clubhouse and the greenkeeper's cottage, but alas is no more) was used as a competition office. The cottage appeared on the Frilford Heath logo for many years until it was demolished.

A Lady Captain's Day - 1950's

In 1980 the County Championships were held at Frilford Heath. Again, the weather was very hot and one lady from Lincolnshire was at least 6 months pregnant. It was wondered if a midwife would be needed on the course.

1983 saw the Curtis Cup squad visiting Frilford Heath for coaching by Vivien Saunders. In the same year, Tracy Craik was awarded her cap for Scotland's Junior team.

In 1984, Rosemary Wilson was Lady Captain and masterminded the inauguration of the Scratch Salver Competition. Tracy Craik was the first winner of the salver; she later turned professional.

In February 1985, Betty Bowen, the President of the Ladies section, died suddenly. She had been a member for 61 years, joining at the age of 15. She attained a single figure handicap, was Lady Captain in 1952 and became President in 1974. In 1982 an honorary membership was conferred on her by the Directors in acknowledgement of her contribution to the Club.

Also in 1985, on a happier note, Pat and Sarah Huntley won the mothers and daughters competition at Royal Mid-Surrey Golf Course beating Peggy Carrick and her daughter Angela Uzielli. Peggy and her daughter had won the competition for the previous 15 years. It was a great win, considering that Angela Uzielli was one time British and English Open Champion and a Curtis Cup player.

The par and standard scratch were equalised on the Red course in 1988.

The 1990s proved to be busy years. County Finals were held in 1990. The South East Divisional Championships were held in 1991. The British Stroke Play Championship was held in 1992. The competition was won by Joanna Hockley with a 5 under par score for the four rounds. In 1992, work commenced on a third course (the Blue course).

During all these years, various alterations had been made to improve the ladies changing rooms (without a great deal of success) and, again in 1992, the room was redesigned once more.

1993 was the Ladies Golf Union Centenary Year. 138 ladies played in the County Shield at Frilford Heath. The winners were Margaret and Susie Glennie who went on to represent Oxfordshire at the finals in St Andrews in October. (This was the first year St Andrews allowed the use of trolleys.) This was also the year when the British Seniors held their Jamboree at Frilford and the South of England Team Squad included Pat Huntley, Margaret Glennie and Brigitte Wilenkin.

August 1994 saw the opening of the Blue course. Joe Skelton, the Chairman, presented Skelton Salvers to the men and women, to be played for every August on the Blue course. There was also another refurbishment of the ladies changing rooms. 1994 was the year in which the ladies entered The Mail on Sunday Competition for the first time. A weekday versus weekend players match was also introduced.

1996 saw Frilford Heath ladies reach the semi-finals of The Mail on Sunday Competition. They were played at Deauville in France, and

Frilford Heath were beaten by Hockley Golf Club, who were the eventual winners.

In 1998, an inspired team of Susie Glennie, Sarah Huntley, Sarah Waugh and Nesta Woolford (with reserves Pat Huntley and Brigitte Wilenkin, and non-playing Captain Jean Lees) won The Mail on Sunday Competition at San Roque in Spain. Brigitte Wilenkin, Lady Captain of the Club had died suddenly on her way to Spain and the team were determined to win for her. Needless to say, all the ladies at Frilford Heath were greatly saddened by the death of Brigitte. She was a popular Captain and had been a stalwart member of the Club.

Also in 1998, the first Junior Girls Open was inaugurated. This was sponsored by the White Horse Contractors (Directors: Ruth and John Binning) who donated a cup, named the White Horse Cup. The event proved to be very successful and is now a popular annual event. The Coronation Foursomes Finals were also held this year.

2000 was millennium year and many interesting events were organised by the ladies. A golf clinic was held by Micky Walker, there was a fashion show, and the Lady Captain, Pam Mathews, organised a special golf competition. Costumes from the early 1900s were worn and hickory golf clubs from that era were used. This proved to be a great success and the men were very intrigued. Pam also arranged for two Millennium Crystal Trophies to be purchased by the ladies section. This competition was to be played for, in pairs, over the three courses during the year.

In August 2000, the English Ladies Open Intermediate Championship was held at Frilford. This proved to be a very successful week thanks to the hard work of the Committee and member volunteers.

In 2001, the British Seniors Jamboree was held at the Club, in which four teams competed representing Scotland, the North, the Midlands and the South. The County Championships were also held in 2001.

In 2002, the club rules were changed and for the first time the ladies had parity with the men. The Lady Captain was now able to attend the General Committee Meetings of the Club.

In March 2002, Mary Carslaw died suddenly. Her father was a founder member of Frilford Heath Golf Club and Mary had been a member since 1927. During the Second World War she and Betty Bowen, who both worked at Headington School in Oxford, used to cycle from the school to Frilford Heath to have a game of golf. She was Lady Captain in 1949/1950 and Lady President in 1990/1991. In November 1997 an honorary membership was conferred on her by the Directors in recognition of her great contribution to the ladies section in the 75 years she was a member.

2004 again saw the County Championships being held at Frilford.

In June 2006, the English Ladies Golf Association South East Division 1 County Week was held at Frilford Heath. It was a very successful week won by Berkshire. The Oxfordshire team and officials, together with all of the volunteer helpers and the Committee were invited to a barbeque at Ruth and John Binning's house to round off this event.

At the beginning of 2007, the number of ladies playing golf was 172. 70 were Silver members of whom 14 had single figure handicaps, and 102 were Bronze members.

Mrs Mary Carslaw

A millenium match in period dress

Oxfordshire Ladies County Golf Association

When the Ladies Section was founded in 1913, Frilford Heath was a Berkshire Club. In 1927 the Ladies Committee applied to be affiliated to the County and were accepted.

In 1952, it was decided that logistically it was more sensible to join the Oxfordshire Ladies County Golf Association and dispensation was given by the Ladies Golf Union for Frilford Heath Ladies to do this. This put Frilford Heath Ladies in the right county when the county boundaries were re-arranged. The men's Captains had always belonged to the Berkshire Past Captains' and decided not to move their allegiance to Oxfordshire Past Captains' at the time of the county boundary changes.

Over the years, Frilford Heath Ladies have been very involved in the county in many ways. Two Frilford Heath members have been County Presidents – Mrs Joan Jackson and Mrs Jane Pezaro who is the current President, elected in 2007.

The office of County Captain has been held by eight members:

1952 Mrs B Knott
1954 Mrs J Hawthorne
1976 Mrs P Huntley
1982 Miss B Notton
1984 Mrs M Glennie
1986 Mrs B Wilenkin
1988 Mrs P Huntley
2002 Miss A Payne.

To date, six members have been County Champions:

Mrs B Knott 1952
Mrs M Glennie 1967, 1982, 1983
Miss T Craik 1984, 1986, 1987, 1988
Miss L King 1989, 1991, 1992, 1995, 1996, 1998, 1999
Miss N Woolford 2000, 2001
Mrs J De Vere Hunt 2002

and 13 members have been County Bronze Champions.

Frilford Heath ladies have also featured very strongly in the Presidents and Captains Inter-Club Trophy competitions, and in the Bamberger Cup competition.

Many Frilford Heath members have held County posts over the years including Handicap Advisor, Representative on the South East ELGA Committee, Treasurer, Secretary, Competition Secretary and Standard Scratch Assessor.

Players have been selected for the 2nd County Team and the Veterans Team.

Originally, Frilford Heath had very few junior girl members, Tracy Craik being the only one of note. Now there is a strong junior girls group who are being coached by the County under an ELGA initiative.

Ladies cups and trophies

President's Cup Given by Mrs Hippisley in 1923. Knock-out competition.

President's Trophy Given by Mrs Pebody in 1950. Knock-out competition for the higher handicap group.

Club Championship Trophy (formerly Scratch Cup) Given by Mrs Belcher in 1931. Silver Division.

Scratch Cup - Bronze Division Given by the Club in 1948.

Andrew Walsh Cup Given by Mrs Andrew Walsh in 1930 for a 2 day competition.

Morlands Rose Bowl - Silver Given by Morland & Co. in 1975. Scratch knock-out competition.

Morlands Rose Bowl - Bronze Given by Morland & Co. in 1975. Scratch knock-out competition.

Greensome Mugs Given by Mrs O'Callaghan and Miss Bowen. Pairs competition to keep interest going throughout the summer.

Bunny Bowl - changed to Copper Cup in 1984. Given by Mrs Greenwood during her captaincy in 1980. Medal round for the higher handicaps.

Granny Shield Given by Mrs Culm in 1976 for the first competition for grandmothers.

Dempsey Cup Given by Captain Denis Dempsey, US Airforce, for a match between the best low handicaps ladies and men, to be played for annually.

Jubilee Cup Given by Lady Cowley in 1935. Handicap limit 24 - Medal round.

Coronation Salver Bought for £25 out of Club funds in 1953. Unrestricted handicaps.

Veteran's Cup Given by Mrs Norridge in 1957. Medal round for players aged 55 years and over.

Ellerie Hoare Cups Given by Mrs Hoare's son in 1961. Foursomes Medal competition.

Dorothy Nicolson Trophy Given by Mrs Carslaw in 1972. (Mrs Nicolson was ladies secretary for many years) for the best four scores in the year in Medal competitions.

Dorothy Acres Vase Bought by the Club (in memory of Dorothy, wife of Jack Acres) in 1967. Best net score in the Autumn Close Meeting, either division.

McGregor Quaich Given by Mrs Elsie McGregor in 1972. Best net score in the Spring Close Meeting.

Bowen Putter Given by Miss Bowen. To be competed for on President's Day.

Skelton Salver Given by Mr. J. Skelton (Chairman) to celebrate the opening of the Blue course in 1994. To be played for every August on the Blue course.

White Horse Cup Given by the White Horse Contractors (Directors: Ruth and John Binning) to be played for at the Junior Girls Open meeting.

Millenium Crystals Bought by the Club in 2000. To be played for over three courses.

Mary Carslaw Memorial Cup Given by the Carslaw family. (Mary was a past President and Captain and her father was a founder of Frilford Heath Golf Club.) First played for in 2002.

Mary Carslaw
Memorial Cup

Lady Captains

There have been lady members of the club from the very earliest days. In 1913 the ladies section was formally instituted and we have records of the Captains of the ladies from 1929.

1929	Mrs F Hippisley
1930	Miss M Forbes
1931/32	Mrs C P Webber
1933/34	Mrs T Evers
1935	Mrs M T Turner
1936	Mrs H F Barge
1937	Mrs W H Linnell
1938	Mrs B C Belcher
1939/46	Mrs E D Harrison-Hall
1947	Mrs M Whitelocke
1948	Mrs C H Dulake
1949	Mrs G Hawthorn
1950	Mrs D P L Carslaw
1951	Mrs A V House
1952	Miss C F Bowen
1953	Mrs J G Osborn
1954	Mrs H D B Goldie
1955	Mrs C B Booth
1956	Mrs H Quelch
1957	Mrs E P Norridge
1958	Mrs J E Knott
1959	Mrs S R Crawley
1960	Mrs C J B Colthurst
1961	Miss D K Nicolson
1962	Mrs B J Mitchell
1963	Mrs P R Stanier
1964	Mrs J B Acres
1965	Mrs J J MacGregor
1966	Mrs J E Alden
1967	Mrs G O M Jameson
1968	Mrs R Wolfe

1969	Mrs T J O'Callaghan
1970	Mrs J C Stephens
1971	Mrs J S Kean
1972	Mrs B Smith
1973	Mrs W F R Hardie
1974	Mrs P Louis
1975	Mrs R G Seaver
1976	Mrs J G Glennie
1977	Mrs J I Whitehead
1978	Mrs P H Skelton
1979	Mrs D Platt
1980	Mrs A H Greenwood
1981	Mrs H Rudkin
1982	Mrs T McGreevy
1983	Mrs R Wilson
1984	Mrs M O'Gorman
1985	Mrs B E Hulse
1986	Mrs P Huntley
1987	Mrs P Burbidge
1988	Mrs M Matthews
1989	Mrs M Normington
1990	Mrs B French
1991	Mrs N Harragin
1992	Mrs D Halsey
1993	Mrs S Bowen
1994	Mrs J Pezaro
1995	Mrs E Christie
1996	Mrs P N Awdry
1997	Mrs S A Wright
1998	Mrs B Wilenkin
1999	Mrs D Cochrane
2000	Pam Mathews
2001	Eileen Wilson
2002	Jean Lees
2003	Beverley Sandys-Lumsdaine
2004	Roma Wilcock
2005	Penny Kendall
2006	Betty Dick
2007	Gill Buck

Lady Presidents

1913 - 1939	Mrs F Hippisley
1949 - 1974	Mrs G Pebody
1974 - 1985	Miss B Bowen
1985 - 1990	Dr I Hardie
1990 - 1991	Mrs D P L Carslaw
1991 - 1996	Mrs R G Seaver
1996 - 2001	Mrs J G Glennie
2001 - 2004	Mrs B Greenwood
2004 - 2007	Mrs P Huntley
2007 -	Mrs B E Hulse

*Miss Betty Bowen - Lady President
1974 to 1985*

Ladies gather in front of the pavilion prior to a competition - through the gate, across the road, the course beckons. 136

Jack Acres
Frilford remembered

It was in the early '50s that two undergraduates, one Oxford the other Cambridge, called at the then Frilford Heath clubhouse - a far cry in both situation and construction from the present palace - desperately hoping that they might manage to beg a round of golf on terms that they could afford. The two were essentially cricketers, but golf also involved hitting a ball around so they enjoyed that too. The trouble on this occasion was the green fee, which had to leave room for a beer or two afterwards - and they were running short of cigarettes, petrol and goodness knows whatever else that was part of undergraduate life.

It was a weekday and there were few members or other visitors about, so they plucked up courage, climbed the steps of the clubhouse (recalled now as a sort of wooden edifice seemingly standing on stilts), ventured in, and went up to a counter which appeared to serve as reception, bar and quite an important part of the club office. Behind it stood a military-looking figure, friendly but a little stern, whom the two young men instinctively knew they should treat with due care and deference, whether he was barman, steward, secretary or whatever. After all, they knew the green fee was beyond their means - five shillings or something prohibitive like that - and this almost certainly was the man who stood between them and the round of golf they dearly wanted to play.

There were, of course, some straight questions to be answered. Who were we? Where from? How come we were there? How much golf had we played? Handicaps? What sort of clubs did we possess? Cricketers? Who for? All that sort of thing. And then the crunch – not without a glimmer of hope. Well, what can you afford?

Pause, while the two had a quick, whispered but audible exchange about the need for beer afterwards and that evening and, oh yes, how many fags did we have left, have we got enough golf balls, and then what about the petrol...

So a deal was struck, one which the two thought was very fair, even though they were going to have to cut down on the smoking a bit or borrow some.

It felt a bit like emerging from one's first job-interview as the two skipped down the steps out into the lovely fresh spring air and set off for the first tee. I can't remember how we played, but I know we thoroughly enjoyed our round. And I recall clearly going up to the counter in the clubhouse afterwards, fishing around in my pocket for the shilling or two we needed for our beers - and there, between us and the military-looking figure, on the counter, were two pints all ready waiting for us. And this time the questions were quite different. Well, how did you get on? Enjoy it? Lose many balls? No question of paying for those drinks - just a dismissive wave of the hand, and a very friendly chat.

That day, and my grateful respect for that gentleman, have lingered in my memory for over 50 years. But it wasn't until I visited the new 'palace' to play in a Seniors match a few years ago that I came face to face again with that kindly military-looking figure. This time I was looking at the portrait of a former Captain and Secretary of the club - Jack Acres.

David Richards

The Professionals

The golf professional is an important and integral part of any golf club. At Frilford Heath the honours board records that in our entire history we have been served by only four professionals. The honours board will be corrected as it is not quite correct!! The first of our professionals is not recorded on the honours board but the club minutes do refer to him so the record can be corrected in this book.

A Pedlar - 1908 to 1913

It appears that there were no committee meetings or minutes kept prior to 1913. The committee records start from January 1913 when the Limited Company was formed to take over the running of the club from the founders. We do not therefore know when exactly Pedlar was appointed but he is mentioned in some of the earliest committee minutes.

In the 19th century and into the early part of the 20th century the role of the professional was quite different to the present day. In addition to the duties that you would expect, the professional had responsibility for the course, there was not a separate head greenkeeper, a situation that is difficult to imagine these days.

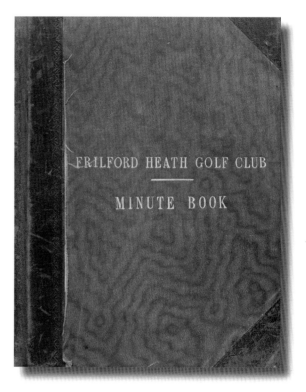

The minutes speak for themselves, extracts are recorded below.

1st November 1913 - *The Chairman reported that Pedlar's conduct had not lately been satisfactory and suggested that the time had arrived when it would be for the benefit of the club to make a change and appoint a Professional and a Greenkeeper separately.*

J H Turner – 1914 to 1952

John Henry Turner joined Frilford Heath Golf Club in March 1914 from Denham Golf Club and quickly established himself as a man of many talents. Not only was he a very good player and teaching professional but he quickly became a pioneer in the world of golf club design and Golf Course Architecture. As if that was not enough, he actually took over as Secretary of Frilford Heath Golf Club during the war years.

An item taken from the committee meeting minutes held on the 1st November 1913 advised that the Board had decided to dispense with services of Mr Pedler whose responsibilities included the dual role of both greenkeeper and professional. The minute shown below taken from the committee meeting held on 6th December 1913 shows the appointment of J.H. Turner as 'Head Professional' with a 'Foreman Greenkeeper' reporting to him.

During his early years as Head Professional at Frilford, Turner organised and played in many exhibition matches. J.H.Taylor, the famous golf course architect, was a regular participant in these matches as the committee meeting minute from 30th October 1919 clearly identifies. It is through this close association with J.H. Taylor that Turner became interested in golf course design. In the following years our own short 9 across the road on the green course and Burford Golf Club were amongst the many courses he designed.

Another great passion of Turners was golf club design. In 1929, he designed an innovative range of iron clubs which were patented and called 'The Grampian range'.

The set ran from one iron through to putter and carried the trademark of a mountain range of several peaks. The primary design differentiator was a thick top edge on each iron's blade into which was drilled a number of holes. Lead weight was inserted into the holes giving added weight behind the sweet spot.

The picture below shows club heads bearing his name and that of Frilford which will be displayed in the clubhouse during the Centenary year.

<u>Professional</u>   The chairman reported that Pedlar had received notice expiring 28th December and that the Directors had engaged J. Turner, Professional of the Denham Golf Club, as from 1st January when his Assistant could commence - Turner himself coming on March 1st, and that they proposed to appoint a foreman GreenKeeper under the "in Professional

To celebrate 25 years of loyal service to Frilford Heath Golf Club a collection by the members resulted in a presentation being made at the Annual General Meeting in January 1939.

During the 2nd world war Turner added to his many talents by assuming the role of Club Secretary. The minute taken from the committee meeting of 2nd July 1949 identifies the appreciation of the then Chairman R.J.Pigott and the arrival of F.V.Spiller as the new secretary.

Following the departure of his son Reg,(who had been his assistant for 25years) to Australia in June 1951, Turner decided to retire. The minute shown below, of the committee meeting held on Saturday 25th January 1952 details his acceptance to retire on a pension of £156 per year after 38 years loyal service to Frilford Heath Golf Club.

SECRETARY: At the commencement of the meeting the Chairman welcomed Mr. F.V.Spiller as the new Secretary and warmly thanked Mr. J.H.Turner, the retiring Secretary, for his valuable services rendered during his term of office. Mr. Turner thanked the Chairman and Committee for their appreciation of his work.

Mr. J.H. TURNER   The Chairman reported that the Directors had interviewed Mr. J.H. TURNER in connection with the letter he had addressed to the Chairman (reported in the minutes of January 5th., 1952) and that he had gratefully accepted an offer to retire on a pension of £156 per year. The question of his successor was now receiving the active consideration of the Board and would be submitted to the Committee in due course.

H C Rule – 1952 to 1979

Born in 1911 Bill was the son of a farmer.

On leaving school Bill became an assistant professional golfer at Guildford Golf Club.

He was married in 1936 in Guildford and had two daughters.

Bills career as a good teaching professional blossomed when he was appointed as the professional at Royal Wimbledon Golf Club.

Bill moved from Royal Wimbledon to Frilford Heath Golf Club in June 1952 where he stayed until he retired in 1979. Whilst at Frilford Bill and his family lived originally in a club bungalow on the Tubney Road and later bought a piece of land and built a house which his wife still lives in today. She is aged 97 and has two daughters, four grandchildren and three great grandchildren. Bill died in 1991.

Dickie Eyles has fond memories of the many hours he spent on the practise area with Bill who was a renowned taskmaster.

Mike Chapman a long standing member of Frilford Heath has the following little anecdote on his relationship with Bill Rule.

I joined FHGC as a relative newcomer to golf in 1976. I quickly realised that if I was to improve I would need to practise and, with this in mind, I booked a series of lessons with the young assistant for Bill Rule to 'sort me out'

At this stage I had never met Bill but had heard that he was a good teacher who spent much of his time with the younger members. At 33 and with a sporting background as a badminton coach I felt that age and fitness should not prove to be a problem for either of us. In the meantime I continued to play and practise on my own and felt that I was making some progress, that is until I met Bill for the first time!

The circumstances were somewhat unusual in that Bill noticed me practising and came up to ask me my name. "Mike Chapman", I replied, and " I don't think we have met before". "That's right I'm Bill Rule and I've been watching you – your bloody rubbish you know". Well having modelled my swing on Tony Jacklin I realised that there was room for improvement but Bill's appraisal stung me to respond with " Yes and that's why I've booked lessons with you from next week and I don't intend to waste my time and money unless you can improve things. Well we will have to see about that" responded Bill and walked off.

The first lesson was more or less a continuation of our first meeting. We started with a seven iron, on the basis that I might just manage to make contact with the ball. After

*BB&O professionals,
Bill Rule second from
right, front row*

thirty minutes Bill's summary said it all. "You can come back next week I think its worth persevering with you, you can at least turn, even though your legs don't work. I'm not wasting my time on all those old farmers who think they know better"

Many lessons later Bill pronounced himself happy, if resigned, to the progress made with a final summary. "Well I've done all I can with you there is no point in any more lessons. You need to go away and really work at it for a while and you should begin to improve after a couple of years. You have all the makings of a golfer who will now and then produce a really low score but I don't think you'll ever get really low – you haven't got the brains for it"

Since then I've got down to six, with Derek's help, and I still have the incentive to try and prove Bill wrong every time I go out......... it's just taking a little longer than I envisaged!

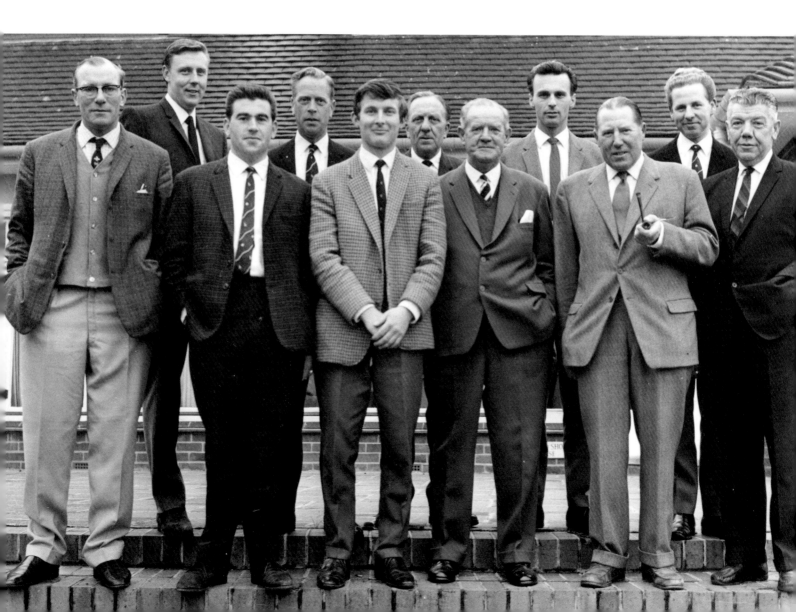

Derek Craik Senior – 1979 to 2001

Born in Forfar Scotland in 1938 Derek started playing golf at the age of 11. He joined Forfar Golf Club as a junior member where the annual subscription was 5 shillings a year. As his golf progressed he joined Carnoustie Golf Club at the age of 16.

After two years of National Service between 1956 and 1958, Derek turned professional and joined Henry Cotton at Temple Golf Club. Tournament golf on the PGA tour followed until the European Tour was formed in 1967. Between tournaments Derek moved to Henley Golf Club as Assistant Professional in 1962 where he progressed to full professional in 1965.

Derek's best tournament finishes were:

1960	8th	Coxmore at Wollaton Park
1962	1st	East of Scotland PGA Championship at Montrose
1965	8th	PGA championship at Princes. (play & tied with Tony Jacklin)
1965	3rd	Bowmaker at Sunningdale
1966	3rd	Skol Lager at Haggs castle – Glasgow

Derek married Marbeth in 1965 and they have three children Tracey, Robin and Derek Jnr. Tracey and Derek Jnr followed in fathers footsteps and became club professionals whilst Robin now runs a successful property development business.

Derek left Henley Golf Club in 1979 to join Frilford Heath as Club Professional where as we know he stayed until he retired in 2001, handing over the Professionals mantle to his son Derek Jnr.

Interesting facts about Derek:

Met Bing Crosby and Bob Hope in 1960 when they played at Temple G.C.
Played in the British Open with Max Faulkner in 1973
Played with an up and coming Amateur Champion called Nick Faldo.
Played alongside Ewan Murray in his first pro tournament in 1972.
He and Derek Jnr knocked out first round opponents Carl Mason and Andrew Chandler in the Sunningdale Foursomes only to lose to two ladies in the 2nd round.
Taught Prince Hiro, Crown Prince of Japan when he was a student at Oxford University.

Derek Craik Junior – 2001 to date

Derek Junior was born in Henley on Thames on 25th May 1970 and moved to Abingdon when his father became head professional at Frilford Heath in 1979. He attended Dunmore Junior School before progressing to John Mason Secondary Modern School.

From an early age, encouraged by his father, Derek showed a natural flair for golf. At the age of 13 he represented Scotland Boys in the Home Internationals and partnered Andrew Coltart in the foursomes. He represented the Berks, Bucks & Oxon under 18 boys and later partnered David Lane of Goring & Streatley in the full team.

In 1986 Derek headed for America on a golfing scholarship to attend the Brovard Community College at Coaco Beach Florida. He returned in 1987 and turned professional in 1988 before joining his father as an assistant professional at Frilford Heath. Qualification as a full professional followed in 1992. Full time tournament golf was the next step for Derek who spent 1996 playing on the Mastercard Tour. In November 1996 Derek became head professional at Chipping Norton Golf Club before eventually retuning to Frilford Heath in April 2001 to succeed his father.

Derek married Lesley in 1994 and they have 4 children – Camilla, Freddie, Georgie and Oscar.

Interesting facts:

Derek and Paul Simpson of West Berks Golf Club beat Luke Donald and his partner in the Sunningdale foursomes.

He finished 3rd in the Brabazon Trophy and won the under 21 section in 1988.

He won the Denham Bowl the last time it was played as a singles event.

In 1992 he won the Southern Region PGA assistants order of merit.

Captains

To be elected as Captain of the Club is indeed an honour. Those who have led the Club over the years are included on an honours board over the Club's main staircase.

Unfortunately the honours board only starts in 1914 when the Club was incorporated as a limited company and it is only from then that a formal committee structure was set up. Records from 1914 are complete, but this is not to say that the Club did not have a Captain from the very start. Indeed, it was reported that the Captain of the Club was a principal attendee at the inaugural exhibition match held in 1909 when The Oxford Times reported thus:

The Lessees entertained the players, the committee and stewards, and a few friends to luncheon in the club room. The Mayor of Abingdon (Mr H S Challenor) presided, and *was supported by the Captain of the club (Mr J T Morland) and others.'*

So apart from those listed on the honours board, we know that the first Captain of the Club was Mr J T Morland. What we have not established, is whether he presided for a few years, or whether there are others who should be listed here and also recognised on our honours board. Perhaps research in The Oxford Times in the Oxfordshire Archives Library would establish the facts. Certainly sport was very well reported then, golf matches were sometimes a feature and Captains may be mentioned.

Perhaps the names of others will be added to the honours board at a later date but for the time being, those listed below proudly represented The Frilford Heath Golf Club as Captain.

75th Anniversary Captain's Meeting 1908 - 1983 29th October 1983

Captains of Frilford Heath Golf Club

1909 - ?	J T Morland	1966	C Stringfellow	
1914	H J Mulliner	1967	W A B Reynolds	
1915 - 1918	C R Scott	1968	J H Fisher	
1920 - 1922	W M Grundy	1969	R Ellis	
1923 - 1924	J L S Vidler	1970 - 1971	H W Acworth	
1925	C Rippon	1972	J T Franklin	
1926	H C S Woodward	1973	J O Skelton	
1927	H J F Hart	1974	P Viney	
1928	N F Henderson	1975	N J Holmes	
1929	O B Challenor	1976	E D Auckland	
1930	J R Pate	1977	A R Thomson	
1931	J A H C Borgnis	1978	R G Seaver	
1932	E G Proudfoot	1979	C S G Phillips	
1933	E K Arbuthnot	1980	R L Faircloth	
1934	H R Peake	1981	D Platt	
1935	Hon. W G Brownlow	1982	R A Mertha	
1936	H A B Whitelocke	1983	M V Morley	
1937	J E Burgess	1984	D Banton	
1938	J W Knipe	1985	C E W Brooks	
1939	A Stradling	1986	P R Clarke	
1940 - 1945	S G K Smallbone	1987	M P Huntley	
1946	P R Knipe	1988	H C Smith	
1947	P R Darby	1989	C R Spalding	
1948	K V Spiller	1990	P Tunley	
1949	D Stevens	1991	M R Partridge	
1950	R W H Mellor	1992	R Nightingale	
1951	J B Acres	1993	P A Savage	
1952	G H Dulake	1994	C B Mainstone	
1953	B B Bowles	1995	G W Hunter	
1954	E J Pether	1996	M C C Morris	
1955	G C Todd	1997	S Styles	
1956	S Cullen	1998	B Edwards	
1957	N B Challenor	1999	C J Davies	
1958	R J Pigott	2000	J I West	
1959	E B Pearce	2001	D C Tester	
1960	A V House	2002	S P Baxter	
1961	C B Bowles	2003	P I Bence	
1962	T S R Fisher	2004	P Dier	
1963	J M Viney	2005	N M Reid	
1964	K N Fisher	2006	P T Reeves	
1965	J H Hooke	2007	D S Manson	

Across left:

Back row: *R L Fairclough, C S G Philips, A R Thompson, E D Auckland, R G Seaver, D Platt, R A Mertha*

Middle row: *N J Holmes, J T Franklin, R Ellis, J H Fisher, C. Stringfellow, H W Ackworth, J O Skelton, P Viney*

Front row: *J H Hooke, N B Challenor, D Stevens, M V Morley, J B Acres, E B Pearce, A V House*

J T Morland

The company Chairmen

Claude Rippon
1912 - 1944

Claude Rippon was born in 1866. He died in 1944 at the age of 78, at Red Lodge, his house in Cold Ash near Newbury; having previously lived in Abingdon. He was buried in Shippon Churchyard with his wife, Belle, who died in 1933. They left a daughter, Dorothy, who died in 1965 and is buried with them.

Claude Rippon's family lived in Oxford and after leaving school he went up to Merton College. As an undergraduate he was actively involved in many activities, particularly those of the Junior Common Room and on the sporting side. He helped the Merton Eight to six bumps in Torpids.

After coming down from Merton he became a journalist and eventually succeeded his father, George Rippon, as Editor of The Oxford Times. His writings of the late 1880s and early 1890s reveal him to be a passionate supporter of the amenities of Oxford. He fought against anything that, in his view, was not in its interest.

Away from work, he played football (goalie) and cricket for Oxford Cygnets. Later he became a referee and was also elected President of the Oxfordshire Cricket Association, a position he held until his death.

It was largely through his energies that Frilford Heath Golf Club was formed and expanded from 18 to 27 holes. He was Chairman at the time the original clubhouse burnt down and so would have been involved with the building of the fine clubhouse that overlooked what are now the 4th and 14th holes on the Green course.

His name is engraved on the Morland Cup, which he won in 1911 with a round of 67.

Claude Rippon was a businessman, a member of the Oxford Canal Navigation Company, Director of the Oxford Super Cinema (now the Odeon, Magdalen Street), co-founder, Director and Chairman of the Alden Press, Director of the company controlling the Cotswold Gateway Hotel at Burford (through his initiative Burford Golf Club was started) and, of course, Chairman of Frilford Heath Golf Club Limited from 1911 to his death in 1944.

Claude Rippon was a man with a great social conscience. He was President of the Oxford YMCA, second President of the Oxford Rotary Club, Chairman of the Rotary District, Mayor of Abingdon for three years, and an elected representative for Abingdon on Berkshire County Council.

He also had many wider interests including photography (an early user of colour) and was a member of the Oxford Photographic Society. He had a keen interest in philately and biology, particularly entomology, and possessed a considerable collection of moths.

Claude Rippon was hugely respected, especially by the staff at The Oxford Times, where he and his wife created a real family feeling at a time when organisations were becoming larger and the personal touch was being lost.

Frilford Heath Golf Club is greatly indebted to him for his vision, hard work and leadership.

William Thornhill Morland
1944 - 1948

Bill Morland was born in 1876. His family came from West Ilsley and both his father and grandfather had been solicitors. The family lived in a large house fronting The Square in Abingdon that had a garden almost reaching the river (today a car park). He married his wife, Dorothy, in 1912 and after a brief period living in the family home moved to 31 Bath Street. They had two daughters born in 1913 and 1916. Later they moved to 53 Bath Street and the house became known as 'Thornhill'. Bill Morland was a devoted father who had endless patience. He was very fond of children, for whom he would devise wonderful and imaginative games in the days before television and with little or no wireless.

The firm, Morland & Son, was established at 33 Bath Street so it was a short walk to work from 53 Bath Street (there was no Stratton Way to cross) and even shorter from number 31. Bill Morland trained with a firm of London solicitors and then joined the family practice. For much of his working life he was the sole partner in the firm, although, after the Second World War, he was joined by Mr Holt, who became a partner. Morland & Son continued in practice until the 1990s when it was taken over by Cole and Cole and closed.

When the First World War started, Bill Morland was too old to enlist at the age of 38, but, in any case, he was rejected because he had a problem with his heart. During the course of his life he had several heart attacks but recovered from them all. He eventually died of jaundice in 1951.

He played cricket, tennis and golf but his abiding interest was golf. He was made a Director in 1913 and also became Company Secretary, a post he held until 1939. In 1944, he was appointed Chairman following the death of Claude Rippon and saw the Club through the difficult period at the end of the Second World War and handed over to Reg Pigott in 1948. He was made an honorary life member of the Club.

He won numerous monthly medals, for which he received silver teaspoons in the same way as winners are rewarded today. Records do not show him winning any major competitions, but some records are incomplete. He presented the Morland Cup to the Club and it is played for annually in the Club Championship.

Perhaps the most extraordinary part of his life occurred in the Second World War. His wife and daughters volunteered for war work but were not taken on. His wife then volunteered to take evacuees from London, Southampton and other major cities and was given the task of taking on expectant mothers. By the end of the war more than 100 children had been born to mothers staying at 53 Bath Street, many of them being delivered by Elisabeth Morland, one of the daughters, although she was not a trained midwife. Many of the mothers came from deprived inner cities so the family also had to acquire clothing for them and their babies. Apparently Bill Morland took all this chaos in his stride and must have supported his wife and daughter in their endeavours. Fittingly 53 Bath Street is now renamed Morland Court; it has been divided into a number of flats.

Reginald Pigott
1949 - 1957

Reg Pigott came from an old Berkshire family that lived in the Faringdon and Hatford area between 1600 and 1860 and then moved to Oxford. He was born in 1892, and educated at Bedford House School in the Woodstock Road. After school, in 1908, he became articled to H S Critchley. He subsequently became a partner in1919 to the then firm of Critchley Ward and Pigott (now known as Critchleys and still associated with the Club).

Prior to the First World War he had joined the RNVR, and he enlisted on 29 September 1914 in the Royal Naval Division. Most members of the RND were sent to the trenches (there was an excess of applications for the Navy) but he was lucky to be allocated to a ship, and ended up as a Lieutenant in the Royal Navy. He joined HMS Humber in Egypt where he remained for the duration. His description of his duties was that of sailing out to shell the Turks before returning to port to play tennis. After 4 years he returned to England, slightly deaf, but good at tennis.

From an early age he had shown sporting ability joining the North Oxford Golf Club. He won numerous trophies there, and also with the Chartered Accountants Golfing Society. He was elected Captain of North Oxford Golf Club in 1923. Living to the north of Oxford, North Oxford Golf Club was very convenient, and he played there a lot, but he never liked the clay.

In 1917, he acquired shares in Frilford Heath Golf Club, and in 1923 acquired some in the proposed Oxford University Golf Club, but this course was never built.

In 1934 he married Helen Shilton (an Oxford dentist) and they lived in Lonsdale Road, but subsequently moved to 35 St Margarets Road.

In the 1920s he continued playing golf at North Oxford but gradually changed his allegiance to Frilford Heath, especially when his nephew Dallas and other friends started playing there. More challenging golf, 27 holes, heathland conditions and a fine new clubhouse would have been a great draw. Philip Darby (see below) was already a member. Reg and Dallas probably gave up their memberships of North Oxford during or just after the Second World War.

He enjoyed riding his Norton motorbike with Philip Darby and took part in trials. They also went to Wengen four winters in succession (1931 to 1934) and skied with the Downhill Only Club. Marriage and two sons ended such frivolities, although family holidays were quite adventurous with a trip to Normandy in 1947 ('to see the rubble') and Canada in 1948. His eldest son, John, was Secretary of the Company from 1958 to 1962 and from 1965 to 1989.

Reg enjoyed the theatre and, like a number of families, had reserved seats (D10/11) at the New Theatre. This meant a weekly trip to the theatre on Saturday nights. He was also a member of the Rotary Club and a Mason.

He took over the chairmanship of the Club after the Second World War and had to face all the difficulties of the time, including rationing, lack of equipment and poor fuel supply. He was also Secretary of the Company from1946 to 1956. The Club survived this difficult period under his able leadership. He loved Frilford Heath, he loved the golf and especially the comradeship.

R.J. PIGOTT

Philip Darby
1958 - 1972

Philip Darby was born in 1899 and died in 1984 having lived all his life in Oxford. His father George was a solicitor's clerk but was given articles and qualified as a solicitor. He eventually formed a partnership with Frank Gray (the son of Walter Gray the developer of the large Victorian houses on the Banbury and Woodstock Roads). Frank Gray died and, in 1925, Philip Darby became a partner and the firm of Darby and Son (now Darbys) began. Philip Darby's mother was an aunt of Dallas Stevens (see below).

The family lived at 67 Banbury Road but later moved to 50 New Inn Hall Street (currently the offices of Darbys). Philip moved to lodgings on Boars Hill and then built a house there, midway between his work in Oxford and golf at Frilford.

He attended the City of Oxford High School and on leaving school worked briefly for the Westminster Bank before being called up for military training. However, the armistice came and the First World War ended. (In the Second World War he was a member of the Home Guard until he nearly died of pneumonia.) He stayed in Oxford and spent three years at St Catherine's studying law.

He enjoyed sport. He rowed for his college. He had a brief interest in riding and he used his hickory skis to go skiing with Reg Pigott (see above). But his great love was golf and in particular playing at Frilford Heath. His regular golfing buddies were Bill Taylor, Bertie Mellor and Jack Rowell. He won the Captain's Prize in 1937. He referred to Frilford Heath as 'nature's cathedral' so he did not see the need to go to church.

In 1932 he married Gertrude Cazalet and they had four daughters, all of whom live in or around Oxford and take a great interest in the Club. He now has nine grandchildren and eleven great grandchildren. One of his daughters, Jane, is married to Pat Minns, a Club member.

Philip Darby was a member of the Clarendon Club and The Oxford Preservation Trust (a committee member on Boars Hill). His great recreational interest outside golf was beekeeping.

Philip Darby was a real gentleman. He was quietly spoken, calm, kind, considerate and he had impeccable manners. He was a stickler for the correct use of language and would have been horrified at today's inclusion of slang in the Oxford English Dictionary. To him it was 'teaspoons full' not 'teaspoonfuls', "there's no such thing as fuls" he would say. 'Very unique', and 'most unique' would make him despair.

Frilford was a place where he relaxed and left behind the cares of the world. As Chairman all he wanted to do was to maintain the Club and improve it where he could and in that he succeeded.

Dallas Stevens
1972 - 1986

Dallas Stevens was born in 1906 in Oxford and, except for a period during the Second World War, lived and worked in or near the city throughout his life. He died at home on Boars Hill in 1986.

His father, George Stevens, was a businessman who not only had a keen eye for opportunities but worked extremely hard. He started a coal wholesale and delivery business in 1896 and it was in this business that Dallas started his working life. George insisted that his sons experience all aspects of the business and so Dallas started his working life filling hundredweight coal sacks and delivering them to houses in the city by horse and cart. George Stevens also started North Oxford Garage and under the umbrella of Stevens & Co (latterly Stevco Ltd), a removal business, a petrol delivery business and a motor spares business.

The family lived at 1 Davenant Road (now a block of flats) and the horses used by the coal wagons were stabled in the fields opposite. Dallas developed a liking for golf from his father who was a prominent member of North Oxford Golf Club and Captain in 1928; the Club being only a short walk from Davenant Road. At North Oxford Golf Club, Dallas won the Scratch Club Championship in 1935 (145), 1938 (146) and 1939 (155). He won the Handicap Matchplay in 1936, 1937 and 1938. He was Captain in 1938. The family moved to 113 Banbury Road just before the First World War.

In the 1920s, with the increasing mobility brought about by cars and looking for greater challenges in golf, Dallas joined Frilford Heath Golf Club. His father probably bought shares in the Company soon after it was formed. Records show that both were members of Frilford Heath by 1927.

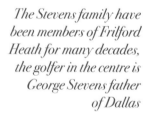

The Stevens family have been members of Frilford Heath for many decades, the golfer in the centre is George Stevens father of Dallas

Dallas married Marion McCulloch in 1933 and they went to live in Owl Cottage, the gatehouse to Lady Singer's Estate at Milton Hill, now the Milton Hill Business & Technology Centre. Subsequently they moved to Boars Hill. They had two sons (Dick is a Director of Frilford Heath) and a daughter.

During the Second World War, Dallas was attached to the National Coal Board in Birmingham organising the distribution of coal nationwide. His younger brother was called-up and was involved in the Abyssinian Campaign.

Dallas became a very keen member of Frilford Heath. He played every Sunday and often 36 holes. He was a regular member of the BB&O Team. His lowest handicap was 2. He won the Harvey Cup in 1929 and 1930, the Cowley Cup in 1930, the Mellersh Cup in 1948 and 1949, and the Club Championship in 1954. Latterly his golfing partners were Colin Booth, John Pether and Arthur House.

Dallas was elected Club Chairman when Philip Darby resigned in 1972. During his chairmanship the opportunity to buy the present clubhouse and enough land to make another nine holes arose. Club finances were not particularly strong so there was considerable debate about the purchase, but with some help from members it was made. The 16th hole on the Green course and the 1st, 9th and 18th holes on the Red course were constructed out of woodland at the back of the house. The members' car park was built on the kitchen garden. The former clubhouse was demolished and the dangerous crossroads made safer by being offset. With some additions, the house became the clubhouse, but considerable alterations have taken place since. Dallas was immensely proud to have played a part in this development.

He was a long-standing member of Oxford Rotary Club. He was involved with Oxford charities, was a member of the Oxford Preservation Trust, supporting their work particularly on Boars Hill. He was a member of Surrey County Cricket Club (he played both cricket and tennis in his younger days) and the Clarendon Club.

He was devoted to Frilford Heath Golf Club and worked very hard on its behalf. To him there was nowhere better and he wanted all members to feel the same.

J O Skelton
1986 - 2007

Joseph Osmotherly Skelton, Joe, a Cumbrian, was born in 1929 and moved to Oxford over 50 years ago. He lived on Cumnor Hill for six years and then Frilford for 30 years from 1963 with his wife, Daphne, whom he married in 1953 and his two sons who were both members of the Club. Joe and Daphne now live in Woodstock.

One of Joe's abiding loves has been golf, which he started playing in 1940, at the instigation of his father. He first played Frilford Heath in 1955, invited by Ken Mitchell, a well-known single figure golfer, who subsequently proposed him for membership in 1956.

Joe read economics at Durham University, where he played rugby and flew with the University Air Squadron, graduating in 1949. After coming down he purchased articles (the system in those days) to a firm of Carlisle chartered accountants and qualified in 1953. His interest was in business rather than professional accountancy. He joined The Wagon Finance Corporation Ltd, a public company, as assistant Managing Director and eventually retired as Deputy Chairman when the company was taken over in 1986. Immediately after retirement he devoted time to his post as Chairman of HPI Ltd.

During his business career he was Chairman of the Finance Houses Association between 1978 and 1980. He was fortunate in having the impressive Margaret Thatcher as his principal guest at the annual dinner in the City in 1978. For a number of years he was a member of the Deposit Protection Board at the Bank of England under the Chairmanship of Eddie George (subsequently Governor of the Bank of England). He was heavily involved with the Treasury in drawing up the Banking and Consumer Credit Acts. He was a committee member of Eurofinas, a federation of banks and finance houses based in Brussels, forming a pressure group scrutinising EU legislation affecting the banking industry. He was a council member of the Society of Motor Manufacturers and Traders.

From the day he joined Frilford Heath, Joe became an enthusiastic member and a regular player. He won a number of monthly medals, the Stradling Cup (with Peter Huggins), the Mellersh Cup and more recently the Past Captains' Cup. He became Captain of Frilford Heath in 1973 and in 1980 joined the Board becoming Chairman in 1986 on the death of Dallas Stevens. Frilford Heath is and will always be a special place for him. He worked tirelessly to improve courses and facilities for the benefit of members and visitors alike.

His contribution to the Club has been immense. The purchase of the adjacent farm and subsequent building of the Blue course was visionary. Apart from being a magnificent golf course it has enabled the Club to host major golfing events whilst scarcely inconveniencing members. Clubhouse facilities have been greatly expanded and improved and this has continued with the building of the Skelton Room and development of conference facilities. Joe instigated the building of the Club's 12 million gallon reservoir, a facility of increasing importance in these days of uncertain weather patterns. But he has also stimulated less obvious improvements, an employees' pension scheme and a system for depreciating club assets being two such measures. As a result of the latter, the Club's golf course machinery is second-to-none. At the outset of his chairmanship he established a firm financial base for the Club and all subsequent developments have been possible because of this.

Joe Skelton's legacy at Frilford Heath is enormous. Past, present and future members are indebted to him for his vision and hard work.

Current Chairman
R D Stevens 2007 to date

Dick Stevens, son of Dallas Stevens (Chairman 1972 to 1986) was born on Boars Hill and lives there still. He became a junior member of Frilford Heath in his teens. After school and National Service he studied for the Natural Sciences Tripos at Emmanuel College, Cambridge. Following university he taught biology at Scarborough College, married his Dutch wife, Rose, in 1966 and in 1967, under the auspices of The Ministry of Overseas Development, went to Kenya to teach A level biology in an all-African boys state boarding school.

After 7 years at the school and having become Deputy Head, he and his family (increased by a son and a daughter) returned to the UK where he became Head of biology at a school in Folkestone. In 1979, the family returned to Kenya and he took up a post as Head of Hillcrest School, an international secondary school run on British lines. He was voted onto the Board of Karen Country Club, a club with a fine golf course and numerous other sporting and social facilities.

In 1989, with their children now training in the UK, he and Rose returned to the UK and he took over running the family business. He and Rose then joined Frilford Heath.

Outside golf and business, Dick 'contains' his garden, plays tennis, races his Laser sailing dinghy at Farmoor Reservoir, sings with The Abingdon and District Musical Society (for whom he runs the publicity), and is a trustee of the Oxford Preservation Trust (he is on its Land Committee and is Chairman of the Boars Hill Branch).

As Chairman he wants Frilford Heath to continue to be the excellent club that it is and where possible to improve and expand its facilities.

The Gold Medal

The 1950s saw the revival of many golf courses following the effects of the Second World War. Membership increased and the improvement and availability of transport allowed the re-establishment of events open to non-members.

The more competitive clubs held 36 hole scratch competitions open to low handicap players. Notable clubs among these were Ashridge, The Berkshire (The Berkshire Trophy), North Hants (The Hampshire Hog) and Temple (Raymond Oppenheimer Bowl). Frilford's Committee decided that with two courses, a 36 hole scratch event would attract a good entry and bring prestige and publicity to the Club.

The first Gold Medal was held in 1961 and won by the Walker Club player David Frame from Worplesdon with a score of 143. Frame won again in 1962 with 147, in 1966 with 145, and in 1968 with 147, a notable achievement. Apart from David Frame's four wins, only J

David Frame

Lawrence (1963 and 1965), Carl Mason (1971 and 1973), M G King (1972 and 1974) and A Rogers (1987 and 1988) have won more than once.

By the late 1960s the Gold Medal was well established on the amateur circuit and was attracting a large entry. The event had always been held on a Sunday but, under pressure from the members, the Committee agreed to hold the event on a Wednesday early in June. The change of date initially affected both the number and ability of the entrants but it has now become a well established mid-week competition.

The well-known player, Warren Humphries, won in 1970 and established a new low score for the event of 138. This was not beaten until Eddie Pepperell from the home club, and then aged 15 years, returned 135 in 2006. Other home club winners were Simon Walker in 1986 with a score of 140, Ashley Walton in 2004 with 139, and Sean Elliott in 2005 with 141.

Winners of the Gold Medal

Year	Winner	Club	Score
1961	D W Frame	Worplesdon	143
1962	D W Frame	Worplesdon	147
1963	J Lawrence	Stoke Poges	149
1964	A G Clay	Worthing	143
1965	J Lawrence	Stoke Poges	142
1966	D W Frame	Worplesdon	145
1967	J H Cook	Calcot	147
1968	D W Frame	Worplesdon	147
1969	A Millar	Denham	147
1970	W Humphreys	Royal Mid Surrey	138
1971	S Carl Mason	Goring & Streatley	142

1972	M G King	Reading	141
1973	S Carl Mason	Goring & Streatley	140
1974	M G King	Reading	139
1975	W J Reid	Fulwell	144
1976	C A Banks	Stanton on the Wolds	142
1977	M D Owers	Maidenhead	147
1978	C Bezer	Lansdown	145
1979	D Rosier	Newbury & Crookham	141
1980	S Scott	Calcot Park	144
1981	J B Berney	Gerrards Cross	146
1982	D H Niven	Newbury & Crookham	143
1983	M Pinner	Ilford	143
1984	A Cotton	Potters Park	146
1985	P Hall	Harrogate	145
1986	S Walker	Frilford Heath	140
1987	A Rogers	Ealing	140
1988	A Rogers	Ealing	140
1989	N Williamson	Hunstanton	139
1990	P Sullivan	Wanstead	137
1991	A Dyer	West Sussex	144
1992	C Rotheroe	The Berkshire	139
1993	S Larner	Colchester	142
1994	A Glover	Pearley Downs	142
1995	M Briggs	Stoke Poges	143
1996	J Kemp	John O'Gaunt	142
1997	J Gallagher	Wentworth	137
1998	R Caldwell	Sunningdale	139
1999	B Smith	East Berkshire	142
2000	S Maynard	Sonning	145
2001	G Harris	Reading	134
2002	K Freeman	Stoke Poges	141
2003	D Richards	Kington	146
2004	A D Walton	Frilford Heath	139
2005	S Elliott	Frilford Heath	141
2006	E Pepperell	Frilford Heath	135
2007	A Glass	Caversham Heath	138

Flora of Frilford Heath Golf Club

The original golf course was constructed 100 years ago on sandy heathland. It was not then considered suitable for agriculture and the free draining soil was ideal for a golf course. This probably preserved what is now an extremely rare habitat from being developed in other ways. The underlying geology is responsible for the soils and the present flora that make up this habitat.

During the Jurassic era, this area of Oxfordshire was part of a shallow sea. The sea levels fluctuated frequently. The Corallian ridge stretching from Oxford to Faringdon is made up of highly fossiliferous rock, created under warm tropical seas. During periods of lower sea levels, sands were deposited, giving rise to sandy beds mixed in with the Corallian layers. This gives a fascinating combination of acid and alkaline soils in close proximity. Frilford Heath is underlain by calcareous deposits and the ground water is therefore alkaline, but there are sandy deposits remaining as a top layer. These sandy layers have increased in depth due to extensive leaching of the limestone, leaving sandy acidic conditions. Also, being on the edge of a ridge there are many springs, these form small rills that gradually drain away and, due to the small gradient, marshy areas are formed. As the ground water is alkaline, the fens are calcareous in nature.

This combination of acid and alkali, free drainage and marsh gives rise to a habitat that is rare in lowland Britain and very rare in Oxfordshire. It was this combination of features, and its consequent flora and fauna, that made the 'Frilford ponds and fens' a candidate for becoming a Site of Special Scientific Interest (SSSI) in the 1960s.

Rough Hawkbit

Since that time a great many changes have taken place at the Club. When Frilford House was purchased in the 1960s a further nine holes were added and a third course was built in the 1990s. The intensity of use has increased enormously. Golf course management has improved to keep pace with the demands of golfers requiring a high standard of playing conditions throughout the year. This course management has not necessarily been to the benefit of the natural habitat, but nevertheless many of the plants recorded 50 or more years ago are still to be found in some localities in the Club's care. From the botanist's point of view the most interesting areas are the practice grounds, the wooded areas, the rough and the surrounding walls.

Marsh Marigold

Trees

One of the biggest changes in the course since the Club was founded is the number of trees present. The old maps show most of the original course area as being open ground. In 2007, there are many more trees, a large number of which appear to be 30 to 40 years old, which would correspond with the alterations made when the club added nine holes in the 1960s. The superb avenue of Lime at the entrance to the Club came into the Club's ownership at this time. There are a few older trees, possibly over 100 years, found around the edge of the estate. For the most part these are native Scots pine and Larch, with the occasional Oak. There are a few exotics such as the Douglas fir (near the 11th fairway, Green course) and Cedar (by the 15th tee, Red course) and the two superb Wellingtonias which together with the Copper beech make a splendid setting for the putting green. These give character to the course.

It is good to see that most of the new plantings on the golf estate are of native trees. On the Blue course, many trees have been inherited, including plantations of alien Conifers, but also of European larch and Scots pine. Sandy wood has a magnificent carpet of native Bluebells at its western edge, where some deciduous trees remain, probably indicating this is a remnant of ancient woodland.

The wet woodland to the west of the 12th fairway of Green course, a nightmare if the golfer's ball finds its way there, is very rich in mosses and lichens and one or two interesting ferns.

one of a line of fine oak to the right of 5th Blue course

The pond at the 9th red course

Shelter belts between the Blue course and the A420 and the Abingdon road at Tubney are a pleasing mixture of native deciduous trees including Hazel, Guelder rose, Cherry, Oak and Ash as well as the occasional Scots pine.

Gorse is extensively used as a break between fairways, with variety given by small copses of Willows, Dogwood and Blackthorn. Older plantings have been incorporated into the planning of the courses, for example the line of mature Oak beside the 5th fairway on the Blue course and the line of Hawthorn between the 3rd on the Red course and the reservoir.

Scots Pine and Larch beside the 11th green, Green course

Colour through the year

The Gorse, used as a divider between the fairways on all three courses is the floristic signature of Frilford Heath Golf Club. Gorse is a prolific flowerer, starting early in the year (January) reaching its peak in spring and early summer, then gradually reducing the output of flowers. There is rarely a period in the year when some gorse is not flowering somewhere.

Yellow and white are the predominant early colours. As well as Gorse, the yellow flowers of Coltsfoot keep popping up wherever the ground has been disturbed. The flowers come out in March and have gone before the big round leaves appear. Spring beauty, a tiny delicate white flower surrounded by a green leafy cup, appears next, and is prolific on sandy soil under trees. The ground is completely covered, then, by the end of May it has all but disappeared.

May sees the flowering of Bluebells. Most of the wooded areas have a carpet of blue, and thankfully the hybrid between the English and Spanish bluebell has not made its appearance. This alien is taking over many bluebell woods in the country and whilst it is a pleasant enough flower, it lacks the scent and the vibrant blue of the native.

During May and June, pink joins the colour scheme. On the Doghouse practice ground and many of the fairways, Cranesbills, Clovers and Storksbills compete for the limited space. In the semi rough, Rockrose and Field mouse-ear continue the yellow and white theme, whilst Bird's-eye speedwell covers large areas with a brilliant blue.

Bird's eye speedwell

Even the pathways and car parks attract special plants. Early in the year Spring whitlow grass covers many such areas with tiny white flowers and, later, Cudweed with its silvery leaves and brown flower heads can be found. Dense silky bent, a rare grass in Britain, can be found on the Doghouse practice ground car park and occasionally on the pathways of the main courses.

Spring Beauty

Later in the year, the purples of Knapweed and Viper's bugloss plus the yellows of Hawk's bits, are found, to be followed by the autumn colours on the trees, especially Birches, Beeches and Oaks. The autumn is also the time when the fungi are most noticeable. Shaggy inkcap stand out behind the 12th green (Blue course). Puff balls abound, which have been mistaken for golf balls nestling in the grass. Regularly found are Parasol mushrooms, which are quite a delicacy, if you are sure of your identification! Less obvious fungi are the scarlet, cup shaped Peziza. These are to be found clinging to rotten branches, if you venture into the wet woods in early spring.

Rhododendron

Inset - Viper Bugloss

Parasol mushroom

Fly Agaric

172

Marshes and ponds

The area in front of the 16th tee on the Red course that stretches across the 2nd hole of the Green course is well known to most members as the Orchid area. The earliest to flower is the Early purple orchid, the flowers are a distinctive purple, but in some years it is a very shy flowerer. More consistent are the Common spotted orchid and Marsh helleborine, with their pink and white flowers. Perhaps not recognised as an orchid is Twayblade, which has two broad leaves cupped around the stem and a tall spike of green flowers; this too is reliable. The rarest of all is Narrow leaved marsh orchid, with its cerise flowers appearing in late May or early June. It has not been seen for a few years, but this does not mean it has gone for ever. The last to flower is the Fragrant orchid, which has a slender spike of pure purple, said to smell of vanilla.

Narrow leaved march orchid

Butterwort is occasionally found here. It is one of the few insectivorous plants to grow wild in the British Isles and it needs open marshy ground to flourish. Grass of parnassus is a beautiful white flower appearing in July but is increasingly rare at Frilford Heath. These plants have all been recorded on Frilford Heath at least since the days of Druce's first Flora, published in 1898. Unfortunately, several plants he recorded as common no longer are so, but it is a triumph that so many do survive.

The ponds by the 6th and 12th holes of the Green course are notable for the Charophyte that grows in them. This a primitive form of plantlife that often looks quite grey as it is encrusted with lime (a sign of the alkaline ground water).

The fen area on the 9th fairway of the Blue course deserves a mention because it is a separate SSSI. Here the pH values are slightly alkaline and plants such as Iris, and Greater tussock sedge are to be found. The latter is interesting in that the tussock can be half a meter or more high and support its own flora. The Iris makes a splendid show of yellow in May and June, to be followed by the purple Himalayan balsam or Policeman's Helmets, another rather attractive alien that threatens to dominate our own native flora.

Most of the small streams or ditches have more acidic water than the fens and support different plants. Many of the sides of these streams are covered by a dense liverwort flora and the stream from the 11th to 12th fairway on the Green course has two acidic lovers that are rare in Oxfordshire: Brookweed and Bog pimpernel.

Marsh Helleborine

The Heath

Fairy Foxglove

Heather on the 7th - Green course

Frilford Heath was renowned for its Heather, but sadly this is in decline. Only remnants can be found in the rough of the Green course, beyond the Abingdon road, and there is a healthy patch in the rough near the 15th green (Red course). Heather requires soil that has low pH values and is low in nutrients. Any drift from the fertiliser put on the fairways will cause problems both by itself and because it encourages the coarse grasses to dominate, which 'suffocate' the heather. Gorse is more tolerant of higher pH values and once established eliminates the other ground flora, including heather. Some attempts are being made to re-establish the native heather and hopefully this will be met with some success. Companions of heather that have been shown to be more resilient are Heath bedstraw, Heath wood-rush and the charming little Pill sedge.

Walls

The walls of the car park are particularly colourful in spring. Alyssum, Aubretia and Arabis are long established garden escapees, which are then followed by Fairy foxgloves (Erinus) and Stonecrops. Ferns, such as Hart's Tongue, grow on the damper walls around reinforced ditches, and mosses abound on boundary walls wherever there is sufficient moisture.

The 'Dog House' practice ground

This has the most natural flora of any part of the golf course because it does not get watered and receives very little fertiliser. It does, however, get mown, mimicking the sheep grazing that once took place. This encourages a rich flora of small plants, many of which seldom exceed 5 or 6 centimeters. The clovers are frequent and include Subterranean clover, which has a white flower and which, when the seed has set, turns its stem down to push the seeds into the ground to ensure the best chance of germination. Others are really inconspicuous, for instance Lesser chickweed and Annual knawel, which are predominately green.

Oxfordshire Rare Plants Register

To be classed as rare or scarce, a species must occur in ten or fewer locations in the county. Frilford Heath Golf course has 38 listed in these categories, of which 21 have so far been identified between 2000 and 2007.

Subterranean clover

Over 350 species of flowering plants have been identified on the Frilford Heath Golf courses (this does not include Bryophytes and Charophytes), and there are sure to be more. Some come, some go, but Frilford Heath will surely remain a very special place for golfers and botanists alike.

Spindle tree

Candidates for the Rare Plants Register

Species name, Latin	English name	Frilford mentioned Druce 1897	FHGC mentioned Bowen 1968	last seen 1986 - 2005	found 2006 - 2007
Aira caryophyllea	Silver hair grass	yes	yes		D
Anagallis tenella	Bog pimpernel	yes	yes		G, R
Anthriscus caucalis	Bur parsley		yes		B, G, R, D
Apera interrupta	Dense silky bent		yes		D
Aphanes australes	Slender parsley piert		yes		D
Calluna vulgaris	Heather	yes	yes		G, R
Carex hostiana	Tawny sedge			1990	
Carex paniculata	Greater pond sedge	yes	yes		B, R
Carex pilulifera	Pill sedge				G
Carex pulicaria	Flea sedge	yes	yes		R
Carex rostrata	Bottle sedge	yes	yes		R
Carex viridula ssp.brachyrrhynchia	Long-leaved yellow sedge		yes		R
Cerastium semidecandrum	Little mouse-ear	yes			G, D
Cirsium dissectum	Meadow thistle	yes	yes		R
Cynoglossum officinale	Common hound's tongue		yes		R, D
Dactylorrhiza incarnata	Early marsh orchid		yes	pre 1986	
Dactylorrhiza traunsteineri	Narrow-leaved marsh orchid		yes	1999	
Danthonia decumbens	Heath grass		yes		R
Dianthus deltoides	Maiden pink		yes	1984	
Dryopteris carthusiana	Narrow buckler fern				B
Epilobium palustre	Marsh willowherb			pre 1986	
Epipactis palustris	Marsh helleborine	yes	yes		R
Eriophorum angustifolium	Narrow-leaved cotton grass	yes	yes	pre1986	
Eriophorum latifolium	Broad-leaved cotton grass	yes	yes	1990	R
Festuca filiformis	Fine-leaved fescue				G, D
Filago vulgaris	Common cudweed	yes	yes		
Gymnademia conopsea	Fragrant orchid	yes	yes	1999	G

Species name, Latin	English name	Frilford mentioned Druce 1897	FHGC mentioned Bowen 1968	last seen 1986 - 2005	found 2006 - 2007
Helleborus foetidus	Stinking Hellebore		yes		R
Hydrocotyle vulgare	Pennywort	yes	yes		
Juncus bulbosus	Bulbous rush			1990	R
Juncus subnodulosus	Blunt-flowered rush	yes	yes		R, G
Luzula multiflora	Heath wood-rush	yes	yes		R
Molinia caerulea	Purple moor grass	yes			B, R, G, D
Ornithopus perpusillus	Bird's-foot	yes			R
Parnassia palustris	Grass of parnassus	yes	yes		
Pedicularis palustris	Marsh lousewort	yes	yes	pre 1986	
Pinguicula vulgaris	Butterwort	yes	yes	1990	D
Plantago coronopus	Stag'shorn plantain	yes	yes		D
Potentilla argentea	Hoary cinquefoil		yes		G
Samolus valerandii	Brookweed				
Schoenus nigricans	Black bog rush	yes	yes	1990	D
Sceleranthus annua	Annual knawel	yes	yes		R, B
Senecio sylvaticus	Heath groundsel				
Spergula arvensis	Corn spurrey			pre 1986	D
Stellaria pallida	Least chickweed				G
Teesdalia nudicaulis	Shepherd's cress		yes		D
Trifolium striatum	Knotted clover	yes	yes		D
Trifolium subterraneum	Subterraneum clover		yes		
Triglochin palustre	Marsh arrowgrass		yes	1990	R, B
Valeriana dioica	Marsh valerian	yes			R
Vicia lathyroides	Spring vetch		yes		
Viola canina	Heath dog violet	yes		1984	

Key to recent finds at Frilford Heath:
B - on Blue course **R** - on Red course **G** - on green course **D** - on Dog House practice field

Centenary project

In the years leading up to 2008 the club was making various plans for the forthcoming centenary. In 2006 the Directors of the company decided to mark the centenary with a significant extension to the clubhouse. The Board approved and commissioned improvements to the existing first floor space above the bar by building a glass 'Orangery'. This has provided additional space for members and visitors with panoramic views across the courses. The area can be accessed from both an external staircase and the current stairs from the bar.

In May 2nd 2007 Joe Skelton retired as Chairman of the company after 21 years at the helm. The Orangery, would be officially opened on Friday 29 June 2007. Joe was invited to do this at a party celebrating his chairmanship and in the presence of the Board, the Captain, Lady Captain and members of the club. David Manson, the Captain, provided an interesting overview of Joe Skelton's achievements in the 21 years he had been Chairman of the Company. For many of us it gave a fresh appreciation of all that Joe had done for the Club. Just before declaring the room open Joe was given a large heavy wooden object which when unwrapped was seen to be a carved nameplate, 'The Skelton Room'. It now hangs above the main door to the room. Joe was delighted with this gesture.

'The Skelton Room' is already being used by members for functions and will be available for outside hire, and of course on a day-to-day basis can be used by the club members.

The courses today

Green course – 1st

To the immediate rear of this green are a stand of majestic Scots Pine which give a superb backdrop for players to view the green. Various types of woodpecker frequently hammer away at the distinctive red bark searching for a meal. Numerous birds of prey also reside in this area with sparrow hawk and kestrel being seen almost daily. One rare visitor has been recorded, although not for some time – the little owl, you may spot him one day.

Green course – 11th

This par four is one of the most visually impressive holes on the course, larch trees and gorse offer outstanding colours throughout the season. The adjacent woodlands offer wonderful protection for specialist hunting birds such as buzzard, kestrel and a rare visitor, the hobby. Much woodland conservation throughout this hole has increased levels of bluebells, wood sorrel and the much loved heather, it is indeed a beautiful hole.

Green course – 18th

Standing on this tee creates the feeling of "home at last" as the clubhouse stands guard over the practice putting green and 18th green. A varied selection of trees, such as pine, birch, holly, copper beech and sequoia, create a wonderful ambiance. An abundance of birdlife flourishes, it is not uncommon for a tree creeper to be seen spiralling up and down the large redwood tree searching for food.

Red – 9th

This magnificent par three has become somewhat of a signature hole on the Red course with the view over the natural pond leading to Victoria Cottage in the background. The pond area has been a magnet for a variety of wildlife including the elusive kingfisher which can often be seen darting across the waters edge as it searches out sticklebacks and other small fish.

Red - 13th

This hole is a demanding sharp dog leg par four over a stream, a testing tee shot for all players. A backdrop of carefully managed gorse helps to frame the hole, the strong healthy growth produces an abundance of stunning yellow flowers which in turn provides the distinctive coconut smell in springtime. On both sides of this hole there are areas which are left to evolve naturally. These areas are a healthy breeding and hunting ground for foxes and stoats.

Red – 18th

Looking towards the green this hole looks every inch the final hole with its stunning views across an undulating fairway. The tight tee shot creates a tempting risk and reward situation for all players. Rhododendrons provide a bright flash of colour throughout the summer months. Majestic trees around the green area help to create an atmosphere of both calm and excitement.

Blue – 3rd

Running through a natural water meadow this superb short hole is flanked by water on both sides offering the player little margin of error. This wetland is one of the most ecologically rich areas on the course supporting an abundance of wildlife, flora and fauna. Breeding birds such as mallard duck, moorhen and coot regularly nest here whilst more illusive visitors like heron and kingfisher are somewhat more difficult to see.

Blue – 6th

Sandy Wood provides the perfect backdrop for this very tough par three. Behind the green, scots pine provide a perfect habitat for an array of bird life to flourish, including the red kite. To the left side of the approach to the green a small pond supports a variety of flora and fauna within the water and around its perimeter, species such as water plantain and reed grass are plentiful. The pond is an enduring habitat for newts, frogs and common toads.

Blue – 12th

This tempting dog leg par four offers all levels of player an interesting challenge with an abundance of gorse and bunkers awaiting the wayward shot. As the dog leg turns hard right, Sandy Wood once again provides a superb backdrop for the heavily undulating green. During the summer

months birdlife is plentiful with yellow hammer and long tailed tits benefiting from seeds and insects, whilst high in the sky skylarks soar singing their distinctive song.

dig for mines
To hold the said
unto the Lessee
years from the
one thousand
unless at the
or fourteen ye
be determined
Lessor six m
writing of his
Yielding for
of this demise
Pounds clear
tithe rent che